# SEARCHING FOR UNCLE LARRY

## A MISSING AIRPLANE MYSTERY

PETER BOCZAR

Copyright © 2016 by H. Peter Boczar
All Rights Reserved

No part of this publication may be reproduced or transmitted in any form or by any means, electronic or mechanical, including photocopy, recording, or any information storage and retrieval system, without written permission from the author.

Cover Design and Formatting by
www.ebooklaunch.com

ISBN 978-988-14331-5-2

Distributed by
MobiShow Ltd.
GPO 4616
HONG KONG

peterboczar@yahoo.com

*For my grandmother
Mary Grasha
Who was always there for me*

# Acknowledgements

Special thanks to the following for their support, encouragement and thoughts:

Paolo Affif, Armyairforces.com, Paul Bayfield, Bill Biegel, Carl Bowen, Patricia Bowen, Dave Edhard, Edit 247.com, Don Ellis, Philippe Espinasse, James Gessling, David Hebbard, Robin Heid, Darrell Hillier, Ted Kaufman, Ralph Love, Ernest Mak, Jean Marsh, Maxwell Air Force Base, Dolores Newman, William Pfeiffer, Stephane Plaine, Michelle Vanderbecq, Claudine Webb, Stanley Webb, Jim Wisman, Lisa Wolters, Sawyer Wolters.

# About the Author

Peter Boczar started writing in the 1970s for magazines and newspapers in Hong Kong, where he also dubbed Chinese kung fu movies into English and made a cameo appearance in the Bruce Lee movie *Game of Death*. As a writer, he traveled extensively throughout the world and notably covered conflict zones in the Middle East, Southeast Asia and Central America.

# Table of Contents

Preface ............................................................................. 1
Chapter One - Grammy ..................................................... 3
Chapter Two - Magic Carpet Ride .................................. 20
Chapter Three - Mom .................................................... 24
Chapter Four - Larry ...................................................... 30
Chapter Five - Training .................................................. 34
Chapter Six - Brazil ........................................................ 38
Chapter Seven - Jungle 101 ............................................ 49
Chapter Eight - Jungle 102 ............................................. 58
Chapter Nine - The Search Begins ................................. 67
Chapter Ten - Congressmen ........................................... 72
Chapter Eleven - Missing Air Crew ............................... 74
Chapter Twelve - B-24 Liberator Bomber ..................... 79
Chapter Thirteen - Radar ............................................... 85
Chapter Fourteen - Initial Plans ..................................... 89
Chapter Fifteen - Ted Kaufman ..................................... 91
Chapter Sixteen - New Plans ......................................... 96
Chapter Seventeen - Psychic Warning ........................ 101
Chapter Eighteen - Spooked ........................................ 107
Chapter Nineteen - Preparation ................................... 111
Chapter Twenty - French Guiana Part I ..................... 114
Chapter Twenty One - Shopping ................................ 116
Chapter Twenty Two - Insertion ................................. 122
Chapter Twenty Three - Trek ...................................... 126
Chapter Twenty Four - Jungle Navigation .................. 136
Chapter Twenty Five - Homeward Bound .................. 146
Chapter Twenty Six - La Bodega ................................. 149
Chapter Twenty Seven - Saül and Saxophones .......... 154
Chapter Twenty Eight - Devil's Island ........................ 158
Chapter Twenty Nine - Music ..................................... 161
Chapter Thirty - Cosmic Commitment ....................... 164
Chapter Thirty One - French Guiana Part II ............. 167
Chapter Thirty Two - Back to the Jungle ................... 172

Chapter Thirty Three - Base Camp Two ......................180
Chapter Thirty Four - X Marks the Spot.....................183
Chapter Thirty Five - A Hole in the Jungle.................186
Chapter Thirty Six - Birds and Bees ............................192
Chapter Thirty Seven - Base Camp Two Again..........194
Chapter Thirty Eight - Back to Base Camp.................196
Chapter Thirty Nine - Departure ..................................199
Chapter Forty - Sea Search.............................................202
Chapter Forty One - Internet ........................................206
Chapter Forty Two - Patricia.........................................210
Chapter Forty Three - Mystery Woman ......................216
Chapter Forty Four - Jean Part I...................................219
Chapter Forty Five - Suriname ......................................221
Chapter Forty Six - Hugh Van Es..................................228
Chapter Forty Seven - Hong Kong Prediction...........231
Chapter Forty Eight - Jean Part II ................................234
Chapter Forty Nine - Boston and Back .......................237
Chapter Fifty - Passing On ............................................242
Chapter Fifty One - Friends & Relatives .....................244
Chapter Fifty Two - The Letter.....................................248
Chapter Fifty Three - Hong Kong Connection..........250
Chapter Fifty Four - Department of Defense.............253
Chapter Fifty Five - Trump Connection.....................255
Chapter Fifty Six - White Knights ................................257
Epilogue ...........................................................................259
Press Links.......................................................................261

## *Preface*

This is a true story. However, some names have been changed to protect the privacy of the individuals involved. Also, given that much time has passed, I have been unable to contact various people to request using their names and don't want to use them without their permission. But that in no way takes away from the veracity of the story.

The world "search" in the title does not do the book justice. It not only refers to the expeditions in French Guiana, South America, where I scoured the jungle for the wreckage of my uncle's airplane. It also refers to searching through the jungle of the U.S. government bureaucracy that anyone faces trying to find answers on such matters.

*Chapter One*
# Grammy

"They never found him, you know," Grammy said.

"Grammy" was what we called my grandmother. On my mother's side.

I grew up in her house with my older sister until I was age five. She took care of us as if we were her own babies. She bathed us, fed us, and even wiped our bottoms on the toilet before we learned how to do it ourselves.

She made great pies. Her apple pies were made with big chunks of apple, but her specialty and my favorite was elderberry pie. Elderberries are a blue-black berry that grow in clusters on shrubs. Some confuse it with a blueberry but the size, taste and texture are unique. Grammy pronounced it "aldaberry." As kids, we scavenged for elderberries on her brother's farm. We brought them back home and Grammy made them into pie. It was great fun and maybe that's what made the pie taste so great. But I later learned that those berry fields were full of snakes and never did it again. I also learned that elderberries had tremendous health benefits but improperly cooked elderberries are poisonous. Obviously, Grammy knew how to cook them or I wouldn't be writing this story.

"Him" was her son Larry. Missing in action in World War II.

She kept a picture of him in her dining room and whenever she caught me looking at it, she reminded me, "They never found him, you know. His airplane was lost in the jungle."

She didn't bother to tell me which jungle and at that age, I didn't bother to ask.

When she caught my mother looking at the picture, Grammy added, "He looks just like Peter."

Larry was my uncle, but I never met him. He went missing on March 1, 1944 and I wasn't born until 1953.

So, the only Larry I knew at that time was his mother's idealized versions of him. His sister, my mother, refused to talk about him, as if she were keeping some dreadful secret safe, so I never learned much about him from her. Many years later, I may have found out why.

However, from the age of five, it was burned into my soul that my lifetime mission was to find him.

Grammy's house in Maplewood, New Jersey, Uncle Larry's house, was the same house that I grew up in. It was small but cozy, and Grammy kept it in immaculate condition. She was fastidious about cleanliness. She had painted all the woodwork white, so she could see the dirt and scrub it away, she explained. She also tended a flower and vegetable garden in a nice backyard flanked by white wooden fences and tall hedges.

The yard was big enough to hang out a day's worth of laundry for drying on long lines that encircled the entire back yard. As kids, we loved running through the freshly-laundered washing and brushing our faces across the sweet-smelling bed sheets and towels fresh from the washing machine while playing hide-and-seek.

The vegetable garden was a product of World War II. It was only a small patch in the back of the yard against the neighbor's property. She called it a "victory garden." It seemed everyone was growing tomatoes, potatoes, broccoli, cauliflower and asparagus during the War to supplement the food supply. Grammy also had a peach tree in the back yard, but the peaches never seemed to measure up to human standards, so she fed them to the squirrels. But I loved to climb that tree. When I sat up in the branches, I felt like I was the king of the backyard.

However, the flower garden was her personal pride. Flowers ringed all boundaries of the property. She had all types of flowers and spent hours nurturing them. I never understood the purpose of flower gardens. After all, you couldn't eat them. Though, as a three-year-old, I once tried eating the petals of a rose. I saw someone do that on a television show.

Grammy never picked the flowers or brought them into the house, but let them live out their full lives in the yard. They were like her children.

She also had a bird house in the garden. Her brother, my Uncle Bill, made it for her. I don't think that any birds lived there because it was my job to shinny up one of the laundry poles that held it about eight feet above ground and pour seed into a tray outside the house where the birds could roost and feed. And I never saw any birds inside. Not even a feather.

She attached another bird-feeding tray outside the kitchen-table window, which also overlooked the yard.

She always kept both stocked full of seed and birds often came there to feed. She enjoyed watching them and called me to the kitchen window whenever they came. Her favorite was the robin red breast.

One day, she turned up from the local toy shop with a plastic "put together" model, as I called them, that required me to paint the bird and paste its pieces together with strong smelling glue you squeezed out of a tube. When I was done, she hung it on the wall across from the kitchen dining table as if it were the Mona Lisa and always made a point of telling everyone that "Petey did that."

"Petey, "Pee Tee," "Peedy" or "Peedy Boy" however you want to spell it, was her nickname for me. If I had to pick one spelling, I'd go for "Petey."

Grammy loved birds as much as flowers, but never kept any as pets. She hung up an antique bird cage in the kitchen, but only for decoration.

One year, she found a lost, injured parakeet hobbling in her garden and brought it into the house, put it in the antique cage and nursed it back to health. For weeks we tried to get it to say "Polly want a cracker" or "Peter" but to no avail. In the meantime, its chirping was driving my father nuts and he just wanted to release it. Grammy refused. Instead, she put an ad in the local newspaper looking for the owner. Fortunately, the original owner saw the ad and Grammy was able to return the bird to her before my father let it loose.

Grammy married Lawrence John Grasha, whom we all called "Pop Pop." He was the grandfather on my mother's side. They had two children, Josephine, my mother, most commonly called "Jo," and Lawrence, better known as "Larry."

Apparently, I was the one, at two or three years old, who gave my grandfather the name Pop-Pop, though no one could tell me why. Maybe because my father called him Pop but the name stuck. It's funny how adults take on the nicknames given to them by children.

I remember many years later, visiting my mom in California with my sister's family, and my three-year-old niece was constantly referring to someone called "Dee Dee". "Who's that?" I asked?

My sister replied that it was what my niece called my mother, because when babysitting her, my mom used to dance a clown doll around her, singing, "Dee Dee Dee Dee. That's how the clown dances." Ironically, she used a cloth clown doll that I had saved from my childhood. Ever since, everyone called her Dee Dee except me. I preferred "Mom" but acknowledged her as Dee Dee in the presence of my nieces.

Pop Pop was born in 1896 and died in 1963 at the age of 67. He was born in Poland, somewhere near the city of Krakow, which was considered Poland's cultural capital. Throughout history, Poland was sliced, diced and betrayed so many times by various governments, notably Russians, Prussians, Germans, Austrians, French, Brits, Americans. It's amazing it actually ever became a country in its own right. At one point, it disappeared from the map. The fact that it eventually reappeared as a sovereign country likely had something to do with the strong spirit of the Polish people.

The history of Poland at that time was essentially an ongoing struggle to protect its sovereignty as a country and its culture as a people. The Poles made amazing cultural and scientific contributions to the world community. Think Chopin, Copernicus, Madame Curie. But after World War II it was betrayed by both America and Britain, who turned it over to the Soviet Union as a satellite state, and it endured the brutal terror that followed. Many Polish army officers were arrested and massacred after World War II because the Russians considered them a threat even though they helped fight the Germans and suffered significant casualties.

The irony is that before the war, the Germans wanted the Poles to join them in an invasion of Russia, but they refused, so Germany invaded Poland as one of its first initiatives in World War II. A German warship visiting the port of Gdansk on a "good will mission" suddenly decided to bomb it on September 1, 1939. That could be considered the official start of World War II.

During the Middle Ages and for many years thereafter, Poland was a safe haven for Jews fleeing persecution from other parts of Europe. At one point, eighty percent of the world's Jewish population lived in Poland. The Jews brutally killed in German gas chambers have been well documented. But ironically, the first people killed in German gas chambers were Polish Christians near the city of Gdansk after the Germans occupied it. The German objective at the time was to get rid of all Slavic people and colonize their lands with ethnic Germans. Poland bore the brunt of that program.

Years earlier when Poland was sliced up by Russia, Prussia, Germany and Austria, Poles living in the German sectors were required to Germanize the spelling of their names and assimilate into German culture. So, my name, Boczar, which is pronounced "Bo Char" in Polish, was Germanized and spelled Boettcher, or Böttcher. I was told by that my family name might have meant "charm" or "magic spell" in Polish but in Russian, it would have meant "barrel maker." The German version didn't seem to have any meaning. Some suggested "butcher" but in German that would have been "Fleischer."

My father's father came from the Austrian sector in the southeast. He was born in 1889 and died in 1957 at the age of sixty eight. He married Anna Dankowska and had four children. Allegedly, the Austrian sector was the poorest part of Poland but milked for the highest taxes. Starvation was common. Although my father's family was awarded a coat of arms some centuries earlier for defending Poland and Austria from Muslim hordes invading from the east, there was no castle or monetary rewards. In fact, my father's father's house was made out of sod. I saw the picture. Although my father was proud to tell everyone we were descended from Polish nobility and show them our coat of arms, most Polish nobles ended up working as servants for the various occupying powers.

Interestingly, when my father's father emigrated to the U.S. he indicated that his nationality was Polish but his country Austria and he was a tailor by profession. We called him Jajee, Polish for grandfather. In Polish it would have been spelled Dziadek. We called his wife Babchee, Polish for grandmother. In Polish it would have been spelled Bacia. I began to understand why my father could speak Polish but couldn't read it.

On my mother's side, Pop Pop's wife and my grandmother, Mary Kwiatkowski was born in the U.S. near Albany in the state of New York. Her family also came from Poland. In addition to English, they spoke Polish at home, though the kids never picked up much because they were addressed in English. Polish was a secret language that husband spoke with wife to keep conversations private from the kids. Another rationale was that it would make the kids more "American" and the thinking was that if they didn't speak a foreign language and they'd do better at school. My father felt the same way and my mother couldn't speak much of it anyway, only aggressive one-liners when arguing with my father. But I would have loved to speak a foreign language and later heard that if you learned a foreign language as a child, you could easily pick up another one later in life.

They said the same about music. If you studied music as a child, you could easily learn a foreign language. However, that was not the case. From the age of five, me and my sisters were all put through piano lessons. Me for almost ten years. Same as my Polish-American cousins. I assumed that it had something to do with Chopin and hated him for it. Piano lessons were very painful for me.

In elementary school we were required to study a musical instrument and play in the school band or orchestra. I wanted to play the cornet, a short trumpet, but the orchestra leader said I didn't have the right teeth for it, so hustled me onto the clarinet, which I never liked. He was Polish so my father took his word as that of God. And I later learned that friends with bad teeth were playing the cornet. Some even had braces on their teeth.

All the cool guys played the cornet or the trumpet. And the cool girls played the flute. The nerds played the clarinet or the violin.

In World War II some of the top fighter pilots during the Battle of Britain were Polish volunteers and many lost their lives. On a visit to London, I was very impressed to see that they were acknowledged by name on a commemorative monument established there in 2005. However, I never read anything about them or other volunteer Slavic pilots in Battle of Britain histories.

One of the top fighter aces during that conflict was a Czech volunteer named Josef Frantisek. Although Czech, he served with the Polish Air Force that was fighting for Britain. Allegedly, his British commanders constantly chastised him because he typically left the squadron formations to attack German aircraft single-handedly. He tallied up some of the most kills in the Battle of Britain and was ranked third among the aces of that conflict.

Pop Pop emigrated to the U.S. in time to avoid World War I. Nevertheless, along with notables such as Walt Disney and Ernest Hemingway, he volunteered as an ambulance driver in Europe during that war.

As a kid, I was a big fan of the "Mickey Mouse Club" TV show. It was on television five days a week and thanks to the theme song, I learned how to spell Mickey Mouse even before I went to school and learned the alphabet. I could sing the ending farewell song *"M-I-C See you real soon. K-E-Y Why? Because we like you. M-O-U-S-E."*

Whenever Grammy caught me watching the show she proudly noted that Pop Pop served with Walt Disney in World War I as an ambulance driver.

Pop Pop was an American patriot. Despite being born in Poland, in World War II, he registered for the draft at age of forty-six.

After the war, Pop Pop became a mason. Not a member of the secret society of Masons, but a bricklayer. He pulled together his own small team of men and worked on houses in the nearby communities that builders targeted for suburban development. Apparently, he saw a business opportunity and bought up some of that land himself before the developers took note of it. Although his family lived modestly, they had a 1949 black Cadillac in the garage, so I assume the land deals paid off.

It was sometimes scary when Pop Pop came home from work if Grammy was out in the yard, because he'd pick me up and swing me around in circles as I screamed for my life and begged to be put down while he smiled and laughed.

That was his way of showing love.

The most fun I had with him was when he took me for a ride in his old, beat-up blue pickup truck to one of the building sites he was working on. The truck was something you'd expect to see in a *"Grapes of Wrath"* movie and I'd bounce up from the seat and hit my head on the roof of the cab every time it hit a bump in the road or Pop Pop slammed the stick shift into a new gear.

When we got to the building site, he'd release me into the dirt and ditches where his team showed me how to break bricks, lay them in a line, apply mortar with a trowel, skim off the excess and make a nice neat indentation in the cracks with a special tool that looked like a long skinny spoon.

My first childhood memories are of Grammy's house, where we lived for several years before my family got our own home.

My father and mother slept in the master bedroom. Grammy and my older sister shared a four-posted canopy bed in the next largest bedroom, where I also slept but in an adjoining crib. And Pop Pop slept in what had been Uncle Larry's room. It was not much of a bedroom. In fact, just a small entry room that led to the home's attic door and stairway. It was only large enough for a small single bed and chest of drawers. No closet space. But Grammy always referred to it as "Larry's room."

The basement was big enough for a good-sized Lionel electric train set layout, which was a Christmas present I had initially received as a three-year-old from my father. We only set it up for Christmas and every new Christmas Dad bought me another train car or other accessory that expanded my line. It was set up on a ping pong table that was covered with green, fuzzy paper which imitated grass.

In the process, I learned how to wire things together and drill holes in the table to feed the wires through. My dad didn't let me use the power drill until I was five years old, but I was pretty proficient with the manual drill and learned a lot about electricity in the meantime. Of course, after Christmas, the table was full of holes and bounced the balls in unexpected ways when we actually used it as a ping pong table.

The basement or "cellar" as Grammy called it, also had an independent laundry room and a small, "canning" room that held shelves of thick-glassed, wide-mouthed, rubber-gasketed "steaming jars" that contained the vegetables Grammy pickled.

Grammy boiled the glass jars in a pan, filled them with raw vegetables from her garden, added some secret liquid, then sealed the jars tightly with a wire arrangement that snapped the tops closed over the rubber gasket. Then the jars sat in the canning room until Grammy decided they were ready as dinner table relishes.

My father loved them and was particularly fond of the small green pickled sour tomatoes while I preferred the pickled cauliflower, which was sweeter.

Although Grammy's house was small, there seemed to be enough room for everyone, including a big Christmas tree in the living room with lots of presents. Christmas was a special time for us. Not just because of the presents, but because we kids dressed up in red flannel pajamas with feet. My father made a point of taking 8mm movies of us coming down the stairs on Christmas Eve to hang up our stockings on the fireplace. Then he repeated the sequence the next morning on Christmas Day, featuring us coming down the stairs to open our presents.

Also, my father's relatives came over for a big feast in the dining room, with folding tables spilling out into the living room to accommodate all the guests. And my father's family had kids my age. I wasn't old enough for school at the time and there weren't any kids my age in Grammy's neighborhood, so it was the big social event of the year for me. Sometimes, my Uncle Stanley, husband of Dad's sister, Aunt Jeannette, dressed up as Santa Claus to give out more presents from a big red sack. And Uncle Teddy, my father's brother, gave us more money than kids our age should have had, but with the stipulation that we put it into a savings account in the bank for college. My aunts and uncles were like mothers and fathers to me.

Of course, these days, you can't put money in a bank account to save it. After a year, the banks will confiscate the funds and turn it over to the state on the grounds that the account is not active. So much for saving for the future.

Unfortunately, my last Christmas in Grammy's house was not a pleasant memory. After typically filming us with his wind-up 8mm movie camera coming down the stairs to open our presents under the Christmas tree, my father dragged me into the kitchen, pushed me down into a chair in front of the table and announced I was not allowed to open my presents until I ate a "proper" breakfast. It was a disgusting, watery soft-boiled egg he dumped into a bowl. It looked like nose snot.

No one came to my rescue except Grammy.

Everyone else was silent including my mother.

For some reason my older sister wasn't required to eat one. She quickly finished the bowl of her favorite cold milk, sugar packed cereal, then ran off to joyfully open her presents. I could hear her excitedly tearing away at the wrapping paper while I was held hostage in the kitchen staring down at the snot-nosed egg.

Everyone felt terrible about my father's behavior, but only Grammy said something.

"Let him open his presents," Grammy intervened. "He will eat it later."

But my father was adamant.

I was also adamant. I sat there in my red Christmas flannel pajamas with feet staring down into the watery snot-nosed egg. There was no way I was going to eat it. I fought back tears and was not going to let my father see me cry. I don't know whose blood gave me this courage. I was only three or four years old at the time but this was going to be a fight to the death. I assumed my fighting spirit came from Grammy's side of the family who were builders, hunters, farmers and mountain men. I always looked up to them. But when they wanted to take me out for duck hunting or deer hunting, my father refused to let me go along.

I always thought about what Grammy's brother Uncle Johnny would do. Uncle Johnny was a hunter and builder. He lived in upstate New York and built his own log-cabin home from scratch. It wasn't what you might think. The inside was immaculate and full of all the modern conveniences. It had a bear rug on the living room floor. Needless to say, he shot the bear himself. He was one of those strong, silent types and I always compared him to the head cowboy in the "Rawhide" television series. I knew Uncle Johnny would not have eaten those snot-nosed eggs.

On the other hand, my father's family came from a long line of tailors, some who were interned in the Nazi Auschwitz concentration camp. They were all Roman

Catholic and had non-threatening professions like tailor and shoemaker, but that didn't seem to matter to the Nazis. The Nazis wanted to "cleanse" Poland of Slavic people and colonize it with Germans. Five of my father's relatives were interned in Auschwitz for no other reason than being a Catholic tailor or shoemaker. Ironically, the only one who survived the camp was a cadet in the Polish Army. But he later took his own life after he got out.

Finally, my father gave me an ultimatum on the snot-eggs.

"You can eat it," he announced. "Or get a spanking."

I opted for the spanking.

He brutally yanked me out of the chair by the neck of my pajamas and slapped me hard several times on my bottom. Fortunately, he was on target. Sometimes he missed and hit the small of my back which was very painful and crippling.

In later years, it was worse cause he used a ping pong paddle. Again, if he hit you with the flat face of the paddle, it was not too bad. But, if he hit you with the edge, it was horrible. Something I could have sued him for in modern times.

After my spanking, I walked away from the kitchen table and looked back to note that Pop Pop had taken away the bowl of snot eggs and eaten them. Pop Pop never let anything go to waste and often lectured me about all the people starving in Poland. So, I didn't know if he was eating the eggs to avoid the waste or helping me avoid my fate to eat them later. But you had to love Pop Pop for the gesture. Either way.

I walked into the living room where my older sister was gleefully opening her presents and not concerned with the drama in the kitchen or the tears now running down my face.

I nursed my wounds, and found my presents under the tree, but that single, stupid moment over a watery, snot-nosed, soft boiled egg at the age of three or four, formed strong opinions in me about my family. I never knew why my father decided to be a jerk on that particularly day or why eating an egg was so important to him. Normally, Grammy cooked me oatmeal for breakfast, sweetened with maple syrup.

However, as a result of that experience, I concluded that Grammy and Pop Pop were the only ones who loved me and were the only ones I could trust. I held that belief for the rest of my life.

So when it came time to look for their lost son Larry, I couldn't say no. It was my turn to repay their love.

While still living with Grammy and not yet old enough for kindergarten, I spent most of my time helping her in the kitchen or the yard, and shopping for food with her around the corner at a small delicatessen and butcher shop or down the hill along Parker Avenue to an A&P grocery store there. For that purpose, she had a two-wheeled basket cart that I helped her drag back up the hill after it was full of groceries.

One of the shops around the corner was a candy store with a counter flanked by swiveling stools. It served ice cream and sodas. In those days, they called it a "soda fountain." If you wanted a Coke, they'd pump out some syrup from a faucet into a cone shaped piece of paper held by a stainless steel stand, then switch it over to another faucet that spewed out soda water and turned it into a Coca-Cola. They also let you mix and match flavors.

There, I became a connoisseur of fountain-mixed Cherry Cokes and chocolate malted milk shakes.

A big treat was when Grammy's brother, Uncle Bill showed up and helped out with the backyard chores. He not only taught me how to use hammers, saws, screwdrivers, drills and pliers but gave me my own set of tools. I was only five years old, but took it all in. He didn't just teach me how to use the tools, but also how to make things. The first thing I made was a mini work bench to keep the tools in.

Sometimes, Grammy loaned my labor to her next door neighbor Mister Masterson to help out with his garden. It was pretty flimsy compared to Grammy's. While Grammy had a beautiful garden with a wide range of colorful flowers, his was mostly weeds and dried out stalks of one kind of plant or another. There were a few tomato plants but none edible in my opinion. Basically, my job was to crawl around on my knees and pull out the weeds. I guess that made him feel like he was tending his garden.

Mister Masterson had a Gorbachev-like scar on his forehead. He said it was from a rifle "stroke," which he received in World War I. Only later in life, I realized what he was talking about. Some enemy soldier in some European trench had tried to bash his brains in with the butt of a rifle.

After learning that, I always felt unsettled that he called it a "stroke" as if it were something soft and gentle like a girlfriend running her fingers through your hair. But his generation always seemed to downplay the extreme conditions and tragedies they endured during the Great War and somehow got on with their lives, not thinking too much about it, not trying to be heroic about it or reliving its past.

The only acknowledgement Mister Masterson gave to his war time past was to march in the town's annual Veterans' Day parade. We all came out to watch and cheer his name as he strode past with the remnants of other comrades in arms that somehow managed to survive that terrible tragedy.

*Chapter Two*
# Magic Carpet Ride

When I was five years old, my family moved into our own home. Pop Pop built it himself and gave it to my parents as a wedding present. It was also in Maplewood and, needless to say, since Pop Pop was a mason, it was all brick.

It was probably the only all-brick house for blocks. Maplewood was a historic town with lots of trees and big parks. Most homes were made from wood and each one was different, unlike the modern suburban tracks with look-alike houses typically associated with post-War II America. Some Maplewood homes were even constructed in the eighteen century and proudly posted the date. One even noted 1776 on its front door.

The location of our house was perfect for a kid growing up. It was across the street from Tuscan Elementary School so I could walk to class in five minutes. That meant I didn't have to get up early in the morning to catch a school bus. It was also just a few blocks away from a large park where I played Little League baseball and Lacrosse. Behind the school was a tree-covered brook where we played out Tom Sawyer adventures. And the neighborhood had lots of families with kids my age.

Tuscan School was named after American Indian Chief Tuscan, whose tribe had once occupied the area. There was a portrait of him in the school lobby, and of course, as kids, it never occurred to us that the government probably ran his people off the land and stuck them on a reservation somewhere. We didn't know any better, but were taught to respect his heritage, and felt proud to be a part of his spirit.

Shortly after we settled into our new home, the front door bell rang. It was a woman selling the *World Book Encyclopedia*. Encyclopedias in the 1950s and 1960s were the Internet of their time. They had all the facts about anything you wanted to know from A to Z and came in leather-bound volumes that looked impressive on a bookshelf. While the saleswoman made her pitch, I flipped through her sample volume. It had great graphics, color pictures, and plastic transparency overlay pages that allowed you to dissect various subjects, notably the human body. The books offered everything that would entice a young enquiring mind. Me and Mom were sold but we first had to clear it with Dad.

Meanwhile, on the next visit to Grammy's house, Grammy made a point of showing me a picture of Larry. She then opened a drawer and gave me a yearbook from one of the technical schools he attended in the Army Air Corps, and a pair of aviator flight goggles like you'd see pilots wearing in World War I biplanes.

"These were Larry's," she noted. "You look just like him. They never found him you know," she added. "He was lost in the jungle."

"I will find him, Grammy," I replied in all sincerity. "I promise." A pretty heavy promise for a five-year-old.

I was still not old enough to enter kindergarten. My birthday fell in December, so I was still only four years old when the September school season started and the school advised my parents to wait until the next year rather than let me be the "baby in the class." Sort of like the orchestra leader telling my parents I couldn't play the cornet. But my father respected authority and my mother wouldn't argue about it.

So, I had plenty of time to make friends in the neighborhood.

My best friend was Randy who lived nearby with two older brothers and two sisters. Randy and I spent most of our time crawling through neighbor's bushes "playing army," shooting at imaginary enemies with sticks for rifles and exploring each other's garages that were typically occupied by junk from our homes rather than automobiles.

One day, while we were exploring my family's garage, I stumbled across some strips of carpet left over from our living room. One of them was big enough for both of us to sit on. Coincidentally, I had just seen a Disney cartoon about Ali Baba flying around the world on his magic carpet. The first thought in my mind was that we could use this as a "magic carpet" to fly around the world and find Uncle Larry.

I convinced Randy to sit on it with me and search for Uncle Larry. I sat upfront in the "driver's seat" and rolled up the front of the carpet to take off. Needless to say, we never physically got off the ground, but our imaginations took us off on a great adventure "flying" over oceans and jungles until my mother broke the spell.

"Get up off that filthy ground!" she yelled at us from the backdoor.

I finally entered kindergarten, but reading lessons did not start until another year in first grade with the Dick & Jane series most notable for the phrase "See Spot run." Spot was their dog.

That didn't get me excited about reading, but when we typically visited Grammy's house on Sundays, Pop Pop would read me the newspaper comics and teach me the words in the cartoons. My goal was to read the comics by myself. Forget about Dick, Jane and Spot.

Additionally, I often flipped through our new treasure, the *World Book Encyclopedia,* to see what the color pages offered. If something caught my attention, I'd get my mom or dad to read it to me.

One thing did.

Helicopters.

I learned a lot just from the pictures. Helicopters could fly and land anywhere. And in the next first grade art class, I used color crayons to sketch a picture of me and my best friend flying in a Sikorsky helicopter looking for Uncle Larry.

When I presented the work to the class, the teacher showed some concern. After all, I was only six years old and already planning an international mission, in a helicopter no less. She must have told my mother about it, because I couldn't find the sketch after I brought it home and assume my mother threw it away.

Ironically, more than 40 years later, when I had sufficient information and resources to assemble a more realistic search, I was dropped into the jungle by helicopter, though not a Sikorsky and not my first choice of transport.

Sikorsky was the helicopter featured in the *World Book* series, so the only helicopter name I knew. Undoubtedly, some shrewd advertiser's concept of product placement. The reputation of the *World Book* haloed their reputation as a helicopter manufacturer. And although I had never been in one, I felt that somehow they must have been the best.

Advertising works.

*Chapter Three*

# Mom

My mother was always a bit of a primadonna.

She graduated from Columbia High School. The family had moved from Hillside, New Jersey where she attended Hillside High School, then transferred to Columbia High School when the family moved to Maplewood. She and her brother, Larry, were only a year apart and very close.

She was involved in the Dramatics Club, which made sense because she aspired to be an actress, but also the Swimming Club, which made no sense because she couldn't swim and was deathly afraid of the water. She also indicated that her future plans were college, but didn't seem to take her studies seriously. When her parents pushed her to go to college, she pushed back.

They sent her to a small school, Keuka College, in upstate New York, which my mother referred to as "Puke Up College." Apparently she was not a model student and her best memory of the place was when she and a few girlfriends threw classroom furniture into the swimming pool one night.

I don't know if she was kicked out of school or her parents pulled her out, but she never graduated. She moved back to Maplewood and got a job as a retail model for one of the big department stores in New York City. I can't say for sure, but think it was Macey's.

I found some of her old studio pictures and must say she was a pretty hot babe at the time. She not only had a great figure but projected a seductive, aloof look that reminded me of some of the sexy screen stars of those times. Although my mother's goal was to become an actress, her parents didn't approve. According to my mother, their sentiment was that all actresses were prostitutes. So they pressured her to stop modeling for the department store and instead she started working in it as a sales clerk.

She met my father at a Polish-American Association networking event she attended with a girlfriend.

"Your father and his brother were sitting at the next table," she related years later. "Their ears perked up when we started talking about golf."

Apparently, Uncle Teddy, the younger brother, who was the more outgoing and dashing of the two, went over to the table and introduced himself.

After he joined the girls, my father followed. Apparently, Uncle Teddy was delivering most of the charm while my quiet, intellectual father wearing wire-rimmed glasses wasn't saying much. Based on conversations with my mom, it seems she felt threatened by Uncle Teddy's advances and thought my father's shyness was cute.

My father was one of two brothers and two sisters. Sadly one of the sisters died at an early age. My father was the only family member who attended college. Newark College of Engineering.

During World War II, my dashing Uncle Teddy was drafted into the Army and shipped off to Europe where he was assigned to an artillery unit. He returned home a nervous wreck. His passion was drawing and photography and he ultimately got a job with a scientific glass company, illustrating their catalogues. Meanwhile, he pursued photography in a makeshift studio in the basement of his Irvington, New Jersey home where the ceilings were barely high enough to accommodate the lights. He specialized in portraits.

My dad was also drafted into the army, but got a stateside assignment, maybe because his brother was already deployed to a war zone. After the war he worked for a textile firm, then a company printing technical manuals and quickly rose to the rank of manager. I think that's what impressed my mom.

"He was so young and already a manager," she once remarked.

Dad and Uncle Teddy both had Polish names. Uncle Teddy was Thaddeus Casmer Boczar and my father was Henryk Peter Boczar. "Henryk" is often thought to be Dutch because of the "ryk" at the end. However, it was the name of famous Polish notables in the arts, sciences, journalism, royalty and government. His mother affectionately called him "Henush."

I assumed that the "ush" at the end was a term of endearment because she called her husband Jan, "Janush" and Uncle Teddy, "Tedush." His father Jan later changed his name to John to make it more American.

I was named after Dad, but my mom hated the name, so I was raised by my middle name Peter and she called my Dad Henry.

Of course, when I signed my name H. Peter Boczar, I always had to explain what the "H" stood for and got more than my fair share of snickers throughout my school years. The teachers couldn't pronounce either my first name or my last and everyone laughed at me when they tried. In junior high school, they seated you based on the first two letters of your last name. Of course, mine was "B-O" bathroom odor. More laughs. So, at a very young age, I developed a very thick skin.

There was always some tension between my mom and Uncle Teddy when he came over. Maybe the regret of marrying the wrong man. Maybe the guilt of a small transgression. He always flirted with my mom. In fact, in later years, he even flirted with my girlfriends. But he loved us kids and we loved him. Every time he visited us, he'd give us a quarter, a twenty-five cent coin that could buy almost a week's worth of candy at that time.

He also bought me a super high-tech single-sideband transceiver after my dad pushed me into ham radio and I passed the General Class license exam. I think it cost $500 which was a lot of money at that time. It was a Swan 500c with one thousand watts of transmitting power, the maximum allowed by the Federal Communications Commission for ham radio operators. It only offered a five kilohertz readout, versus the top of the line Collins models that offered a one kilohertz readout, but that was good enough for me.

The readout sensitivity was critical because it allowed you to dissect your way into a jammed bandwidth and connect with a signal. One kilohertz was the gold standard.

Ham radio, also called amateur radio, allowed licensed operators to connect on various short-wave radio bands. In some way, it was another sort of Internet in its time. The encyclopedia gave you A-Z information, however ham radio allowed you to talk with anyone in the world.

The first time I used the Swan, I connected with someone in Angola, Africa.

At the same time, you were very restricted about what you could talk about. Allegedly, some Big Brother organization monitored your transmissions, so the conversations were mostly about what equipment you had and what antenna you were using. I wanted to learn about people and their lives, not their antennas. So I quickly lost interest.

More importantly, Uncle Teddy taught me photography and how to develop and print film in his studio of sorts in the basement of his Irvington home where he and my father grew up in a three-story apartment house. He lived on the second floor with his mother. His sister and their family lived on the top floor and a renter lived on the first floor. We were always warned as kids not to run around the floor so we didn't disturb the renter below. I'd only wish that some of the upstairs neighbors in my future apartments around the world disciplined their kids in the same way.

Later, the photo skills he taught me allowed me to get a position as a photographer for my high school newspaper. Additionally, he gave me the keys to the darkroom in his basement so I could process film whenever I needed to. That got me started in newspaper work and I later secured my high school paper's position as feature editor, which launched my career into journalism.

Sadly, Uncle Teddy was killed by a drunk driver who ran a red light and mowed him down as he was crossing the street in a retirement community.

I didn't hear about it until a couple of years later. I blame my mother for that who never got along with my aunts and uncles and didn't communicate with them.

Uncle Teddy was my father as much as my brother so this hurt me deeply. Like all uncles, he was also a best friend that you could share secrets with and get advice on how to manage family affairs.

It was a devastating loss for me.

*Chapter Four*
# Larry

Lawrence "Larry" Grasha grew up with his older sister, Josephine, father Lawrence and mother Mary, in the nice, older suburbs of Maplewood New Jersey about twenty miles from downtown New York City.

Maplewood was a town of about 20,000 people at the time. As noted, Maplewood had tree-lined streets, great parks and good public schools, including Columbia High School.

Uncle Larry was born July 13, 1924 and his sister Josephine was born February 3, 1923. They were very close not just in terms of birthdays but also in terms of their relationship. They graduated Columbia High School only one year apart. Larry in 1942 and Jo in 1941.

Larry's last address was the family home on 109 Orchard Road.

Columbia High School for years turned out students destined for the top U.S. universities - Harvard, Yale, Princeton and Columbia. The latter no relation. Larry was a good student but declined to pursue higher education. He was anxious to go off to war and afraid of "being left on the sidelines."

For some reason, he was not eligible to enlist after graduation. He was seventeen years old but would be eighteen in a couple of months. Enlistment age. But he needed a consent letter from his mother for some reason. He pleaded with Grammy for the letter, allowing him to sign up.

Grammy never forgave herself for signing the letter and blamed herself for his death the rest of her life. I never learned what the letter was all about.

At the time, if you enlisted instead of waiting for the draft to catch up with you, you could pick the service you preferred, provided you qualified. Larry was very keen on the Army Air Corps and becoming a pilot. The entry qualification for the Air Corps was a height and weight restriction of six feet and 180 pounds. At five-foot ten inches and 154 pounds Larry was accepted. However, once you entered the service, the follow-up testing and qualifications were very rigorous, especially in terms of eyesight and eye-hand coordination if you wanted to be a pilot. Fail some tests and you could just as easily end up being an Army Air Corps cook.

On October 17, 1942, he enlisted in the Army Air Corps. The Army Air Corps was later re-established as the Army Air Forces. But the names were used interchangeably in various documents and I was never sure which to call what. On October 18, he sent a letter home indicating that he was at Fort Dix, New Jersey. He enlisted for the duration of the war as did all other enlistees.

Despite the horrors of World War I, most of the survivors did not talk about it, so the next generation had no perspective of the reality of combat. They all assumed they would come back to glory and girls. Also, it was not just considered as a national duty, but a rite of passage to manhood. Mothers would taunt other mothers if their son was in the service but the other's was not.

According to Larry's high school yearbook of 1942, his nickname was "Sharp" and he participated in the Junior Night Scenery Construction Committee, the Senior Play Construction Committee and played intramural football. Not the activities I'd expect from someone eager to run off to war. I would have thought he'd be playing varsity football, basketball or baseball.

I was also never sure how to interpret that nickname. He was a good-looking kid with strong features, an athletic physique, good grooming and a determined, intelligent look in his eyes. But, "Sharp" didn't seem to fit with the choir-boy image Grammy depicted. And my mother claimed he had lots of girlfriends. But I don't know if that meant actual girlfriends or just hopeful admirers.

The only one he mentioned in letters home was Jean Marsh, a freshman when he was a senior. I don't know if Larry ever officially proposed marriage to Jean but everyone considered her his fiancée.

They met through my mother and she lived just around the corner from Larry at 14 Boyden Avenue.

In the meantime, Larry got lots of postcards and Christmas cards during his enlistment from various women with names like Topsy and Marybelle, so I never knew what to make of that.

But Larry gave Jean a set of his cadet aviation wings. She was the only girl he ever took a picture with and, as noted, the only one he mentioned in his letters home. So, I assumed Jean was "the one."

The statistics of World War II never cease to amaze me. Millions were not killed but tens of millions. Approximately, seventy to eighty million soldiers and civilians died in the war. The Soviet Union suffered an estimated twenty-seven million deaths or fourteen percent of its population. About fourteen million were from Russia and seven million from the Ukraine. Poland lost some six million or about seventeen percent of its population.

Meanwhile, Britain lost about half a million and the U.S. some four hundred thousand, but both less than one percent of their populations.

Germany lost around seven million, an estimated seventeen percent of its population, depending on who is doing the math. Japan gave up about three million souls or about four percent of its population, and China lost twenty million or about three percent of its population.

The numbers were staggering but the joke was that the British would fight to the last Russian and American.

*Chapter Five*
# Training

After induction at Fort Dix, Uncle Larry shipped off to Atlantic City, New Jersey, for basic training. Atlantic City is a coastal town in the southern part of the state.

It was noted for its beach, boardwalk and amusement parks. Not a bad place to start out in the military.

But one month later, he was sent to Sioux Falls, South Dakota where he was trained as a radio operator. I found it very ironic that, as a kid, my father got me into ham radio also known as "amateur radio." It allowed civilians to quality as shortwave radio operators within certain restrictions. But the frequencies you were allowed to operate on let you reach out to the world.

I noted that the military radio training program required Larry to pass a Morse code test of fifteen words per minute. That was pretty fast. At that speed you started to hear whole words rather than single letters. To get my Novice Class license, I only had to pass five words per minute. But that restricted you to continuous wave also known as "CW" or Morse code transmissions when we all wanted to pick up a microphone and talk with people around the world. That required a General Class license, thirteen words per minute in Morse code, and an advanced radio technology exam.

It was not that easy. I failed the Morse Code exam the first time. I couldn't even write at a speed of thirteen words per minute. But one of the old hands told me I should not try to print the letters, but write in script and not to worry about crossing the "tees" or dotting the "i's" until the end of the transmission.

That was good advance and I passed the code test the second time, but then failed the advanced radio theory exam. Finally, on the third try, I passed both and got my General Class call sign which allowed me voice communication over a wide range of frequencies with other ham operators all over the world. My call sign was:

WA2FXG

It was not a great call sign from a marketing standpoint.

Foxtrot, X-ray, Golf in radio speak. I want to know who came up with the idea of using "golf" for the letter "G?" On the contrary, it seemed like everyone else was able to make up cool names with their call signs.

I recalled hearing transmissions from WB2RER, the *Red-Eyed-Rooster*. I think he was based in Texas and everyone wanted to connect with him.

There was no clever, catchy slogan I could think up for mine. The X was a problem. What did it offer besides x-ray and xylophone?

But my radio training gave me another connection with Uncle Larry. Why did my father push me into it? Before then, I didn't know shortwave radio and ham operators even existed. I just wanted to be a Boy Scout, which my Dad opposed for some reason, so I never even got to be a Cub Scout. And apparently, as part of your radio operator qualifications in the Army Air Corps at the time you were required to build a radio transmitter from scratch.

Did my father secretly expect me to connect with Larry on the air waves? I didn't even know he was a radio operator until many years later when I got the government files regarding his missing airplane. I assumed he was a pilot.

From Sioux Falls, Larry shipped off to Harlingen, Texas to attend aerial gunnery school.

At first, I didn't understand why a radio operator would be shipped off to gunnery school, but later learned that radio operators were cross-trained as mechanics or gunners. Larry was cross-trained as a waist gunner.

A waist gunner was someone who stood in the middle of the aircraft's fuselage, manning a machine gun poked out of the window. At high altitudes the air was freezing cold and the slip stream forced more frigid air through the window freezing your butt off and icing your goggles. The gunner manned a .50 caliber machine gun which could easily tear up an attacking enemy fighter, if he actually managed to hit it. However, given the motion of your aircraft as well as the fighter, the gunner would be lucky to hit the enemy a few times for every two hundred rounds of ammunition expended.

Meanwhile, he was trained to do everything blindfolded and in thick gloves because that's the condition he'd be facing when his goggles and body froze up at high altitudes.

Larry spent the rest of his training in Harlingen, Texas until he was assigned to a bomber squadron at Langley Field, Hampton, Virginia in August 1943.

The 3rd Sea Search Attack Squadron, 1st Sea Search Attack Group, 1st Air Force.

In Air Force parlance, a squadron typically consisted of a number of similar airplanes. A number of squadrons made up a Group and the hierarchy continued upwards from there. All I know is that, many layers up, he was ultimately attached to the First Air Force.

At least Larry passed his radio training and would not be a turret gunner squashed into a cramped fishbowl shooting at enemy fighters with no more protection than Plexiglas windows. Though Plexiglas was a bit more bullet proof and flak-resistant than the plane's aluminum fuselage, getting out of the turret to bail out with a parachute was a struggle.

Larry was frustrated because he never saw combat. His group at Langley Field in Virginia was tasked with two missions. The initial mission was to patrol the coastline, find German submarines trying to infiltrate U.S. waters and destroy them.

In Larry's words, "Blow 'em out of the water."

Most Americans would not even consider the Germans a threat on home soil, but it was very real. Americans tended to think that they were pretty invulnerable to the war. However, U-boats were tasked to blow up shipping and shipyards as well as any other coastal military installations. Additionally, they placed commando teams on shore who were assigned to travel to the heart of America, blow up factories producing war materials and wreak havoc anyway they could.

A number of places along the coast had high lookout towers. They were not lifeguard stations keeping an eye on swimmers, but structures manned by troops keeping an eye out for German submarines.

The second task assigned to Langley Field was to test various advanced technology systems developed by American universities, primarily MIT and Columbia, to specifically find submerged U-Boats.

*Chapter Six*

# Brazil

Although Larry was only flying coastal missions, you could see that they took their toll.

The picture of him first entering the service was of a smart-looking, bright-eyed, happy robust young man. Only a year later, he was a sallow scarecrow with sunken cheeks and eyes. It looked as if he had aged forty years. You could easily tell that he was not getting good sleep or good food.

Yet he wrote letters to his family every week that were always upbeat and positive. Typically, they ended with the signature line, "Keep 'Em Flying."

Unfortunately, the letters he got in return from his mother and sister typically complained about home-front living and lack of money. In response, he regularly sent a chunk of his military pay check back home.

One of his last letters broached the idea that he might be transferred to Brazil. He claimed that he'd be doing the same job, looking for submarines off the coast and regretted the fact that he was not going to be part of the action in Europe. He told his family he already had several buddies down there, the food was good and the lifestyle relaxed.

He further noted that he'd be reporting to a twenty-seven-old colonel and that he'd only be doing "experimental" work, nothing combat related. I don't know if he was being sarcastic or trying to impress his family that he would be working with a senior officer.

His commanding officer, Colonel William C. Dolan, would have been about 37 at the time so I don't know whether that was a typo or there was another 27-year-old colonel involved. Also, the Sea Search units at Langley were disbanded in April 1944 and Dolan was killed in a B-24 crash en route to England February 1945 allegedly carrying some high technology that would bring an early close to the war there.

The key bases for American fliers in Brazil were Belém, Natal and Fortaleza. They were primarily transit stops for aircraft en route to Europe or Asia. To avoid long ocean passages, planes being shipped from the U.S. to Europe were sent either by the North Atlantic or the South Atlantic routes.

The northern route went from Maine to Newfoundland, Greenland, Iceland, then Britain. Alternatively, the planes went directly to Britain from Newfoundland. Also, Presque Isle, Maine to Scotland. I found it strange that the pilot's data claimed his last assignment before Trinidad to Belém was Presque Isle.

The southern route went from Florida to Borinquen Field, Puerto Rico, Waller Field, Trinidad, then Val de Cães Field at Belém , Brazil, sometimes stopping at Atkinson Field in Georgetown, British Guiana. In 1943, French Guiana switched its allegiance from the German puppet state in Vichy France to the Allies, so that offered another possible stop as well as a radio checkpoint. The first stop in Brazil was Belém just across the Amazon River and the planes then flew onto the east coast towns of Natal and Fortaleza, where they then jumped across the Atlantic to Senegal, Liberia, Sierra Leone or the Gold Coast, a former British colony, now known as Ghana. Then they'd head to North Africa or points east. Sometimes they stopped in the mid-Atlantic at bleak Ascension Island.

En route, they'd keep a watchful eye for German submarines that were trying to infiltrate the U.S. via South America and the Caribbean.

However, there was also an airfield in Amapa, a province just northwest of Belém on the west side of the Amazon inside Brazil. Allegedly, a number of planes crashed around there. One year I got a letter from someone in Brazil who indicated that gold prospectors had found a B-24 in that area. Unfortunately, it didn't have the same tail number as Larry's plane.

Interestingly, a lot of these routes were pioneered by Pan American Airlines pilots pursuing commercial routes and some of the lesser airfields such as Amapa were refueling stops. In fact, the U.S. government actually paid Pan Am to develop these air fields under the guise of commercial aviation knowing that they'd be important for military purposes in the future.

The British offered airfields in its colonies throughout the Caribbean such as British Guiana, Jamaica, Antigua, St. Lucia, Trinidad. However, they came with a price. Allegedly, for use of these airfields, the British required the U.S. to provide them with 50 naval destroyers, even though the flights were already providing Britain with much needed supplies and protecting their Caribbean assets from submarines. Also, the U.S. had to invest considerable sums upgrading these airfields to make them suitable for heavy bombers such as the B-24. So much for our British allies.

The southern route was considered safer because it offered better weather and you could navigate along the coast. Also, there were radio stations in British Guiana, Dutch Guiana and French Guiana along the way.

Once you reached Africa, you also had easier access to the theaters of war in Europe, the Mediterranean and Asia. It was also critical to reaching China and India after the Japanese disrupted Pacific air routes passing through Midway and the Wake Islands.

U.S. President Franklin Roosevelt flew the southern route to attend the Casablanca Conference in 1943 to plan ongoing WWII strategy.

At the end of February 1944, Larry's plane flew from Langley Field, Virginia to Morrison Field, West Palm Beach, Florida, where they stopped for a break before flying to Borinquen Field in Puerto Rico, then onto Waller Field in Trinidad. On March 1, 1944, they would fly from Waller Field onwards to Belém, Brazil.

During his stop in Florida, Larry repeatedly tried to call home over two days and throughout the evening but the phone didn't pick up. I don't know where Grammy and Pop Pop were, but his sister was out and about with her girlfriends, watching movies and going shopping. No surprise to me. Whenever, I tried to call home from school for an emergency like being sick, my mother was out shopping or lunching with her friends and nobody answered the phone. Alternatively, the phone was busy for hours while she gossiped with girlfriends. As far as my father was concerned, she only needed to be back home by four o'clock to make dinner.

When I was in elementary school, my mother was often not home for lunch and the doors to the house were locked. So, I showed up at the neighbors, soliciting for lunch, or getting myself invited to a friend's house for a meal. I was surprised that my friends actually got hot meals for lunch, whereas I had to settle for a peanut butter and jelly sandwich even when my mom was home. She was often passing me on to different neighbors for a peanut butter and jelly sandwich. One of the worst experiences was when a neighbor's mom fed me a peanut butter, jelly and cream cheese sandwich. Those three ingredients were just not meant to be together at the same time.

Overall, it was an acceptable solution to my mother, but humiliating for me. If I complained about it to my father, I got a spanking.

Meanwhile, I learned how to break into the house though the side door or back porch and make myself a peanut butter and jelly sandwich on stale bread, washed down with Coca-Cola. But sometimes when I got into the house, the inner doors were also locked. So I needed to figure out how to get through them. Sometimes I dug out the locks with a rusty nail from the garage. But when my father found out, he was livid. So most times, I pulled myself up over the back porch gutters onto the roof and got in through my parents' bedroom window which was typically open. I just needed to kick in the screen, which gave in easily.

I did daily pull ups on Tuscan school's outdoor pull up bars to train for this.

It was more acceptable to me than soliciting friends and neighbors. At least I kept my dignity. On the positive side, I think I held the record in my elementary school and junior high school for the number of pull ups, and in junior high school I was the only one in my gym class who could do the peg board up and down. The musclemen in the class, who couldn't even get to the top peg hole, let alone get down again, attributed it to the fact that I was a skinny little runt. I attributed it to pulling myself up the back porch gutters.

If my mom was forced to pick me up at school because I was sick, she complained to my father and I also got a spanking. But the spanking's were pretty mild compared to what came later. My father would rip off his belt and strap any part of me showing, including my face. Sometimes, right across the dinner table. My mother and sisters said nothing. When I was older, I'd grab the strap and yank it out of his hand. I never threatened him with it but never gave it back to him and put it in the garbage can. Somehow, that hurt his feelings.

When I went off to high school, I often stayed at Grammy's house. I could take the bus or ride my bike there. Her house was just a short walk from my high school and I felt safe there. I could do my homework, watch my favorite TV shows and she never stopped feeding me. I slept in Larry's room.

Once I went off to college, I never came home except for two nights to get my tuition check during the Christmas break. To my amazement my parents didn't understand why I wouldn't stay there for the holidays and why I didn't want any presents.

Larry's last letter was written February 25, 1944 and read as follows:

*Dear Mom,*

*Please excuse the delay in writing, but have been very busy for the past couple days. I have been trying to call you for two days, and no one seems to be home every time I called. I called about eight o'clock one night and then six the next night. I am leaving the field very shortly, and will try to send my things tomorrow by express. We have our final inspection tomorrow, and I guess the next day we take off. We will be in South America shortly. I do hope we land in a half decent place. They consider that overseas, and I probably will get an A.P.O.*

*number. I think it will be in Brazil, but exactly where I don't know. From what I hear it's very beautiful down there, and I am just dying to see it. Don't worry mom because it won't be combat work, it will be some experimental work that some 27-year-old colonel assigned us to do. I will write and let you know how everything turns out, I am still not sure of going. I am counting on it, because it will be something new and hope everything turns out ok. How is everything back home, I do hope everything is all-right. Jean expects to be home this coming Saturday. Did you hear anything of Ray Hugg, I haven't heard from him in a long time. Well mom guess that's all for awhile, give my love to all and "KEEP 'EM FLYING"*

*Love Larry,*
*PS. Don't Worry.*

Then he called his girlfriend, Jean Marsh, who was the last person to speak with him before he disappeared. I was not aware of her name at the time. However, when I later found Jean, Larry told her he was on his way to Italy, but didn't want the family to know about it. He told her he'd call them when he arrived in Italy and tell them everyone was fine.

Meanwhile, the pilot, James Buchanan also called his family. He told them that he was on his way to bomb Romania. That synched up with Jean's story because Italy was the staging point for the low level, suicidal bombing raids on the German oil-controlled fields in Ploiesti, Romania.

Napoleon once said that armies march on their stomachs. But in modern times, they marched on oil. The Germans had devised a way of creating oil from coal but still relied heavily on natural oil fields to feed their armies. And apparently, Romania supplied the bulk of their oil.

If Uncle Larry made it to Italy, he probably would have slim chances of surviving the Ploiesti raids in Romania.

The major push on Romania actually came one year earlier. The aircraft flew from Libya and descended on Romania at smokestack levels. But apparently, there were a number of navigation errors and things did not go as planned. Many aircraft did not make it back.

Larry's plane made it to Puerto Rico then went on to Waller Field, Trinidad.

However, that's where the plot thickens. According to sources, the plane was not fit to fly. Allegedly the pilot noted that several of the plane's engines had been tampered with and he refused to take off unless they were replaced.

Engine tampering was nothing new. Spies, sympathizers, opportunists, whoever, working on U.S. Army Air Force bases were often found sabotaging airplane engines. It was simple. All they needed to do was put iron filings or ball bearings in the fuel tank.

As a kid, I was often told by the bad boys in my neighborhood that they'd sabotage cars just for fun by putting sugar in the gas tank or siphon out the gas and sell it to neighbors. I think that's when the auto companies came out with gas tanks with locked lids.

However, the local base commanders on Trinidad were not sympathetic to the pilot or the crew. According to sources, the entire flight crew was marched into an aircraft hanger and told that if they didn't fly that airplane on that day at that time, they would all be court-marshaled.

Research indicated that other aircraft were also pushed to fly with faulty engines. But they were lucky.

Separately, in various reports, the plane was referred to as HYBRID. Was this just a radio call sign or an indication that their plane had been modified to carry and operate some advanced technology?

One thing notable about the B-24-H model was that a gunner's turret was added above the bombardier's position in the nose to deal with head on attacks. So, I don't know if that meant "Hybrid."

Unfortunately, I was not able to locate the local commanders or even the commanders of my uncle's squadron, even though I had their names from various documents. Given all the time that had passed, they were most likely no longer alive.

So the plane took off in reasonable flying conditions and according to the official records, they reported by radio they were sixty miles off the coast of British Guiana, on course, and everything was fine.

However, everything was not fine.

First of all, a number of sources indicated that the cruising speed of the B-24 was about 200 miles per hour.

Second, based on the distance from Waller Field to Belèm and the projected time of arrival indicated by the flight controllers, their average cruising speed would have been about 160 miles per hour. This was recorded in the Missing Aircraft Report.

Third, Waller Field to Georgetown, British Guiana was five degrees. Do the math. Five degrees times sixty nautical minutes per degree times 1.12 miles per nautical mile meant they had only covered about 330 miles over two-and-a-half hours according to the MACR. This meant they were flying at about 135 mph. So, if the expected cruising speed for the B-24 was 160-200 mph then, in my mind, there were engine problems. Either some engines were out or some not running on full power.

The fact that the pilot reported everything was fine was "pilot talk" in my mind. Both combat and commercial pilots are trained to be optimistic, non-emotional and solution oriented. I've know a number of pilots and even when they are crash landing a commercial jet because of fuel problems, all the chatter is positive, non-emotional and task oriented.

Additionally, I found it very suspicious that the actual radio logs were missing from the plane's official documents and government archivists made excuses as to why they couldn't be found.

They claimed that radio logs were filed according to the squadron number so couldn't be found because Uncle Larry was no longer attached to a squadron but Organization/Project AQ7A, which nobody seems to know about.

Their next scheduled radio check-in was Paramaribo, Suriname, which would also be their first point of contact upon reaching the coast. It was about 140 miles away, maybe one hour of flying. Even if all the engines went out, they would probably have been half way there. According to the official documents, they never checked in with Paramaribo and when their plane didn't show up in Belém, search aircraft were sent out to look for them.

However, the search didn't start until one day later because the various bases in the area were arguing about who had jurisdiction over the search. By then the plane would have already sunk to the bottom of the ocean and any survivors in life jackets would have been scattered across the sea by the strong Guiana current and likely dead from exposure to the elements.

The official reports suggested a lot of aircraft were sent out to look for them, but bottom line, they were late so it didn't matter. They were killed by bureaucracy.

One source indicated that other aircraft on the route wanted to turnaround and look for them, but were denied permission. Was this just more military bureaucracy or a direct order to cover up a secret weapon they were carrying and let it sink into the ocean?

*Chapter Seven*
# Jungle 101

As I got older, I forgot about Larry. I was focused on school and getting into a good university. However, for whatever reasons, I was drawn to forests and jungles and wanted to be an expert in outdoor survival. I couldn't explain why. It was just a feeling I had and typically followed my feelings. I didn't even remember Grammy telling me that Larry crashed in a jungle.

After high school graduation, I persuaded my friend Dan to explore the American Virgin Islands in the Caribbean. This would be my first entry into jungle survival. But I was a bit naive. I assumed we'd get off the airplane and walk into the jungle. Also, Dan had since broken his wrist and had a cast on his arm, but was willing to go anyway.

We flew there on Eastern Airlines and arrived at the main airport of Charlotte Amalie, St. Thomas, in the middle of a city with no place to go.

We asked people where the jungle was and mostly got smirks and laughs. Obviously, we should have done more research in advance. Fortunately, we met someone who told us there was a national park on the island of St. John and gave us instructions on how to get the ferry there.

I had visions of living off the land and sea, survival style, and a friend from Maplewood loaned me his spear gun. Meanwhile, I bought a machete from the local camping supplies store and a "U.S. Navy survival knife." It was advertised as being able to "do the toughest jobs under the most adverse conditions." It had a black steel blade, a handle made from rings of leather, a leather pouch and a pocket that included a sharpening stone.

We arrived on St. John early evening with the sun already going down and popped into a local bar by the waterfront to grab a bite to eat and ask where we could pitch our tent. The locals said that the national park was on the other side of the island and if they found us sleeping on their property they would kill us.

We thanked them for their advice and started walking up the road away from the town. As soon as we felt we got away from the town and no one was looking, we made a dash directly up into the hillside though the scrub.

It was grueling. Although it was evening, the temperature had not cooled down and the heat and humidity were unbearable. Additionally, the scrubby plants grabbed and scratched us all along the way. Also, the slope was not forgiving. We slipped and slid much of way. Maybe one hundred feet from the road, we felt we were sufficiently hidden and set up camp although our tent was bright orange.

It was a rough night. We wanted to sleep inside the tent for protection from bugs, but had to set it up on a rocky slope so it was not very comfortable. It was like a sauna inside the tent and the rocks we slept on did not make for a nice mattress. Fortunately, we were still tough kids who could put up with it.

The following day, we slogged our way up and down the roads and stumbled onto a beautiful beach called Hawkesnest Bay. We immediately dropped our gear and ran into the water. It was rejuvenating.

Then we put on our bathing suits, pulled out our snorkeling gear and enjoyed the beauty of the coral reef. The water was crystal-clear and bath-temperature warm. However, no sooner did we think we found paradise than some guy in a uniform showed up and said we couldn't camp there. He saw our tent. We needed to go to the national park several hills away. He also noticed my spear gun and said that if he saw us using it, he'd have to take it. It was not allowed.

Fortunately or unfortunately, we got a tip from some folks that showed up on the beach. They said if we wanted to find a paradise-quality jungle, we needed to go to Tortola in the British Virgin Islands.

But we thought we'd first try the national park. Fortunately, we hitched a ride in a pickup truck or it would have been a grueling hike in the heat and humidity up and down unforgiving hills.

But the park was a big disappointment. We were just assigned a spot as in a trailer camp. It stank of outdoor toilets, but we figured we'd stay for a couple of days to get our bearings.

This was not the adventure we were looking for. So, after a day or so we took the ferry to Tortola, but found ourselves in another dirty town with no place to set up camp. The locals said paradise jungle was on the other side of the island. The only way to get there was by boat.

So we went down to the waterfront and found someone with an open runabout who agreed to take us and pick us up several days later. However, there was some misunderstanding because he didn't take us to the other side of Tortola, but to another island called Jost Van Dyke.

We were dropped out of the boat in waist-high water near the town's garbage dump and told this is where we could camp. Additionally, the boatman said that we could get water from the rainwater barrels in the village down the beach.

But as the boatman took off, he warned, "Beware of Freddie." He is a bad man. Bury your money before you leave your tent."

Great. Here we were in a paradise garbage dump and had to watch out for a bad guy named Freddie.

Nevertheless, we set up camp along the beach, had a dinner of freeze-dried camping rations and the cool offshore breeze blew the bugs away and allowed us a good night's sleep.

The next day, after a light breakfast, we went snorkeling in the bay. Like Hawkesnest Bay, the water was crystal clear, bathtub temperature and the variety of tropical fish was amazing. We swam through schools of many brightly colored fish like you'd only find in a pet shop aquarium.

However, my attempts at securing dinner with the spear gun were fruitless. I could fire it into an entire school of fish around me, but as soon as they'd hear the spear release, they bolted.

I couldn't hit anything with it except sea urchins settled on the bottom and didn't realize they were edible. Years later, I ordered one in a Chinese restaurant baked in the half shell. They had the taste and texture of egg custard and were quite nicer than the bland, slimy sushi version you get in a Japanese restaurant.

I was later told that my mistake was aiming the spear gun like a rifle when I should have been pointing it at the fish as if I were pointing at them with my finger. However, my neighbor's spear gun was pretty massive. It had two rubber bands and forward and rear hand grips. It was meant to be shot like a rifle at big fish.

However, the next day when we encountered a shark off the reef, I couldn't get it loaded. It was too much effort to pull back the bands against my stomach.

As the shark circled me I back-pedaled and desperately tried to load the spear gun and keep it between him and me. The rubber bands were very tight and the butt pushed its way as far into my stomach as it would go. I couldn't get it loaded. I later learned that these high-powered spear guns required leg rests for leverage. Fortunately, the shark swam off. I was later told that you couldn't shoot a shark with a spear gun anyway because their skin is too thick and the spear would just bounce off and make it mad.

The next day, we met Freddie.

He showed up offering drugs and prostitutes. When we declined both, he decided we were not the kind of tourists he wanted. I made the mistake of coming out of the tent with my spear gun. It wasn't loaded and I didn't make any aggressive gestures at him with it, but wanted to show him that we could protect ourselves.

Big mistake.

The following day, we decided to walk down the beach past the village and over a hill to the main town on the other side. The villagers smiled and waved at us as we passed them along the beach.

The village on the other side of the hill was more developed and offered a beach bar along a stretch of sand called White Beach. The owner showed us around and pointed out the foundations of what would be small bungalows for tourists and visiting yachtsmen.

But when we got back to the camp, the spear gun was gone and there was a goat's skull on our tent post. I kidded Dan that it might be some sort of voodoo spell that Freddie cast on us. But he didn't find that funny.

Nevertheless, I shipped it home as a souvenir and was surprised it got through U.S. Customs, even though I noted on the shipping form "one goat skull."

But the villagers no longer welcomed us, presumably since we declined to buy their goods and services. And the next time we went to the village to fill up our canteens with water, they said we couldn't take water from the rain barrels any more. Getting fresh water then became a commando mission.

Dan and I would snorkel up to the beach in front of the village. Then Dan ran ashore to get chased by the villagers. As he distracted the locals, I sneaked around the back of their huts to collect rain water from the barrels, then disappeared back into the sea.

We knew this couldn't last. Anyway, we got bored just snorkeling and hanging about and were happy to see the runabout show up two days later to pick us up.

On schedule, the boat picked us up early in the morning, which promised flatter seas and took us back to Tortola. We immediately caught the next ferry back to Charlotte Amalie. Dan had enough and decided to catch the next flight home, while I went back to Hawkesnest Bay on St. John's. Dan offered me the tent but I decided it would be a burden and planned to sleep under the stars.

Of course, that's until it started raining and I ended up sleeping in the smelly lavatories behind the beach for protection from the weather.

The next day, a group of kids showed up on the beach. Their fathers were diplomats and they seemed to know their way around the region. They indicated that if I really wanted a jungle experience, I needed to go to Haiti or Suriname. I tried to get more information out of them, but they brushed me off when I declined to smoke pot with them.

At that point, I decided to try another island and took a seaplane to St Croix. It was a twelve seater. It started on land, then rolled down a ramp into the bay. Once it flopped into the water, the pilot cranked up the wheels by hand and started the engine. After a bit of radio chit chat, we were off.

After a short ride, the plane belly flopped into a bay along St. Croix, then the pilot cranked down the wheels, and drove us up a ramp under prop power to an airstrip. But, again I found myself in a city with no place to set up camp. I got some ideas from the locals and hitchhiked to a nearby beach. However, the driver suggested that the beach was very dangerous at night and I should spend the night at his house. That sounded a bit too weird, so once again, after a meal of freeze-dried camp food along the shore, I thrashed my way through all the prickly bushes to hide out for the night.

At least this time, I was able to lay out my sleeping bag on flat ground. However, during the night, I could hear cars drive up to the beach accompanied by laughter, screams and boom-box music. Obviously, it was the happening place. Meanwhile, the mosquitos were all over me. I pulled my T-shirt up over my head, covered my arms with another shirt and prayed it wouldn't rain that night. However, I couldn't breathe that well so cut out a hole for my nose. Needless to say, my nose was full of mosquito bites.

The next morning, I went back to the beach where I made a fire and cooked a freeze-dried meal but decided that I had enough and decided to go home. I took the next seaplane back to Charlotte Amalie. However, I missed the flight connection back to New York and was stuck in the city for the night.

I decided to sleep in one of the seats in the airport check-in area, but was slammed awake by a security guard banging his baton on the bottom of my boots saying that I couldn't stay there. He was not sympathetic that I had missed the flight. He offered to put me up in the jail for the night, but I declined.

Instead, I walked down the street along a chain-link fence. On the other side I saw a beach and it looked like a good place to sleep. When no one was looking, I climbed over the fence and started to make myself comfortable, however, after a short time, it started pouring rain and the only refuge I found was in a small low-rise shack protecting some kind of pump. It was not big enough to stand up in, dogs were constantly sniffing around, inspecting me, and it smelled of urine. I squatted down and tried to make it through the night. It seemed like this entire trip I was sleeping in toilets. I suddenly appreciated the plight of homeless people and realized that having a home is everything. Someplace where you can sleep with security. I don't mean at your friend's or relative's place where they're bored with you after a week and kick you out, but a home of your own. Even if it's only one room.

Meanwhile, the blades of my Navy survival knife and camping machete were severely corrupted from the salty sea water and the handles corroded. I brought them home, but ultimately threw them away. I regretted that. They would have been nice mementos.

Many years later, I was sailing around the Caribbean on a chartered yacht and we stopped at Jost Van Dyke's White Beach. The beach bar was still there and the bungalows were finished. Additionally, there were villas up in the hills. Ironically, the back wall of the bar was decorated with goat skulls. I asked the owner if he remembered two white boys who had camped down the beach many years earlier.

"Of course," he replied. "One had a cast on his arm."

That would have been Dan.

"And what about Freddie?" I asked.

"We chased him off the island," he explained. "He was a bad man."

I also realized the importance of planning and rehearsing your mission as well as your equipment. The happy-go-lucky, serendipitous approach taken by most of my generation at the time was an idealistic fraud.

Dan and I weren't that naïve. We had checked out our gear during a weekend camping trip in the hills of New Jersey before the Virgin Islands excursion and I quickly learned that my pack did not have the right harness. There weren't many choices for hiking boots in those days.

At the time, hiking boots were essentially the same as work boots and not designed for stomping up and down hills. Blisters were the norm. Ironically, blisters were accepted by hikers at the time as the price you paid for going into the forest. At the end of the day, you typically burst the blister bubbles with a fire-sterilized needle, doused the wound with stinging alcohol and put a Bandaid on it, ignored the pain and just kept walking.

*Chapter Eight*
# Jungle 102

I was still obsessed with survival training, notably in the jungle, and becoming an expert at it.

Based on the recommendations I got in the U.S. Virgin Islands, I felt that Haiti was my next stop on the jungle tour. I looked into the possibility of going to Suriname, but Haiti had direct flights from New York City, where I was a university student at the time.

I wrote to the U.S. Embassy in Haiti's capital Port-au-Prince for more information. I asked them not only about jungle camping but also about the security situation. I actually got a letter back from the U.S. Embassy. It was very encouraging about my visit and made some suggestions about where I might go. All very diplomatic.

However, Haiti was famous for voodoo rituals and the Tonton Macoute, paramilitary thugs who went around beating up or killing opponents of the regime, often in the ugliest ways. They were recognized by their thick sunglasses, which they wore even at night. They were most active under president-for-life "Papa Doc" Duvalier, but also under his successor and son "Baby Doc" when I was there. Whenever I saw guys with dark sunglasses get out of a car, I went the other way. Also rumors of human sacrifices at voodoo rituals were not uncommon.

So I started to prepare and tried to learn from my Virgin Islands experience.

The most important item on my list was boots. When hiking anywhere, you're on your feet all day long and the only way out of a long walk into the forest is a long walk back out.

After some research, I bought U.S. Army Vietnam jungle boots from a military surplus store in New York City. Although not very attractive, they proved to be a great boot. The heel and front were black leather while the green high-top sides were canvas reinforced with nylon strips. They had a thick, black, hard rubber grooved sole with a strip of steel embedded in it for protection against stepping on something sharp like a punji stick. The high top gave great ankle support and the leather was soft enough so that it didn't require any breaking in unlike most new boots and shoes. They never gave me blisters.

At the same time, I bought a U.S. Army jungle hammock. It was a combination of hammock and tent. The hammock portion had a canvas bed and the tent-like top was a lightweight tarp to protect you from the rain. Mosquito netting formed the open sides with a zipper on the bottom so you could enter the hammock, then seal yourself inside.

I tried it out by stringing it up between the top of the door and one of the window frames on the other end of my room. Although, it bent your back in half, I assumed it was something I just needed to get used to, then it would be comfortable.

However, I never fully tested it out by spending the night in it, indoors or outdoors. I would learn more about hammocks when I first used it in Haiti.

I also bought a new backpack with padded straps and marched around the streets of New York City with it full of books to make sure it worked for me.

I also planned my entry better. I made a reservation at a small pension in Port-au-Prince and spent several days there to orient myself and acquire additional information. I didn't speak any French, but found a thin book in a local shop titled *"Creole for English Speaking People."* It was a great find, and I immediately tried to teach myself the basics.

French Creole is a cross between French and the local native language. It is a simplified version of both languages that allowed basic communication between the French colonials and locals in former years. But more on that later.

As I explored the streets, a cheerful, young Haitian attached himself to me. I'd say he was my age, well-dressed and spoke perfect English. I was wary of his company, but he shooed away the train of beggars that started to follow us looking for handouts.

So I hired him for a day more as a bodyguard than as a guide. He escorted me around town and suggested we meet after dinner to show me the "nightlife." He waited for me outside the pension, then took me to a small concrete box-like structure with a corrugated roof that spewed music through a cloth door. Inside, we sat down at the rudiments of a table with wooden benches and he ordered a bottle of rum. When the bottle arrived, it was only half-full. You paid based on how much was left in the bottle after you finished your drinks.

I then had my first encounter with voodoo beliefs. My guide grabbed the bottle, pulled the cork out and spilled a gulp onto the dirt floor.

"Why'd you do that?" I asked.

"To appease the *loa*, the spirits," he explained. "You must let them drink first or they will be angry with you and cause you trouble."

Voodoo, also spelled Voodou or Voudoun with or without a capped "V" was a belief system that was imported with the slaves from Africa. I never fully understood it, but appeasing spirits and casting spells on people seemed to be a major part of it. Making blood sacrifices, primarily chickens and goats to the "Baron Samedi," a short guy in a top hat with a tail coat also seemed to be a key part of the ritual worship. Apparently, the Baron was a powerful spirit because he was in charge of digging your grave. If he decided to dig your grave you would die. If he didn't, you wouldn't.

In America, voodoo was most popularly known for the "voodoo doll," a cloth figurine that you stuck pins in to torment your enemy.

It was also known for zombies, known as the "living dead."

As we were sipping the rum, I asked my new friend if he believed in zombies. According to the literature, a zombie was a dead body brought back to life or a "re-animated corpse" and enslaved to the person that did it. Quite frankly, I never understood the difference.

"Yes, I have seen them," he replied.

"Where?" I continued.

"In the sugar cane fields," he explained. "The masters give them some drug which makes them work very hard. They never get tired and eat very little. But they can go crazy, take people and eat their flesh."

Sounds like cocaine and investment bankers I thought. Years later, I learned that the drug used might be some sort of fish toxin, which put the subject into a catatonic state. If he survived the poisoning, he was "raised from the dead" and slave-like obedient to the person who had administered it, because he became dependent on the drug. Again, I thought about cocaine and investment bankers.

Some sources indicated that the toxin was associated with blowfish meat the Japanese called fugu. Some restaurants in Japan specialized in this but had to be licensed so they didn't kill their customers. Throughout the years, there were a number of deaths from fugu poisoning. I didn't get it. Why would you eat something that could possibly kill you? Apparently, the idea was that the fugu master would leave a bit of the poison in the meat that would give you a special kind of psychedelic high.

Ironically, when we were kids on the New Jersey shore, we used to catch a lot of blowfish. My grandmother on my Dad's side, Babcie, use to fry them with onions and hash brown potatoes. Nobody died. And nobody got high. Grandmothers seem to know how to do these things. Just like Grammy who used to bake poisonous elderberries into wonderful pies. Obviously, all these exotic chefs had something to learn from grandmothers.

Later, when I was working in the corporate world, I was assigned an assistant from Haiti. Nobody wanted to work with him so they assigned him to me. I typically got assistants that no one wanted to work with. He obviously wasn't a zombie because he didn't work very hard but often glared at me wild-eyed suggesting I should beware the power of the *obeah*.

*Obeah* was the catch-all word for the magical charms and spells practiced by voodoo priests.

On those occasions, I typically looked back at him impassively, unimpressed, unthreatened and suggested that he invoke the power of the *obeah* to get his work done. After I told him I had been to Haiti and drank rum with the *loa* spirits there he stopped the theatrics. Several months later, he left the company and died of cancer at a very young age.

Based on the opinions of my guide and the hotel managers, I needed to go to Cap Haïtian, a town on the northern coast, if I wanted to have a jungle experience.

So I took an all-day bus ride north and checked into another small but comfortable pension, which was run by an unmarried, older German gentleman. I thought I saw several shotgun shells on a shelf behind the reception desk when I checked in, but when I looked the next morning, they were flashlight batteries. My paranoia started to act up. Did he notice me notice and replace them? I wondered what he was doing in Haiti of all places and what he did in World War II. Was he a fugitive from war crimes? Was he avoiding Interpol? Was he doing medical experiments on the natives? Did he escape from a sunken U-boat with a hoard of gold?

But I didn't pursue these questions with him though I was curious to know his story. He was impressed that I spoke some German and gave me a nice room.

I told him about my search for the jungle and he directed me to a dirt path on the edge of town.

"It will take you to a bay," he explained. "But you must get there early in the morning, because you need to take a boat across the bay to the beach on the other side. There are also two trees growing close together where you can put up your hammock."

The next morning, I found the path and began my hike. It quickly took me into a tropical forest, but the trail was well worn and unobstructed so I didn't need to use my machete. It went up and down a few hills, but overall, it was an easy hike. When I got to the top of one steep hill there was a small break in the growth and I could see a beautiful bay down below.

I got down to the beach, where I found a small wooden boat with an outboard engine and man waiting there almost as he was expecting me. For one dollar, he took me across the bay and I arranged for him to pick me up several days later. I don't remember exactly. Maybe four days.

As soon as I got across the bay, I strung up my hammock between the small trees that were there just as the hotel owner had indicated.

But there was no jungle. Just high razor-sharp grass and the kind of scrub I had encountered in the Virgin Islands. Conceptually, the jungle to me was supposed to be a Garden of Eden where you could survive off the land and minimally eat fruit from forbidden trees.

I pulled out my machete and found that hacking my way through the grass was not that productive. When I tried to machete my way through the dense vegetation behind the beach, the grass just bounced back at me laughing. Obviously, I didn't have the right technique, but was able to find enough dry wood to start a fire and heat up one of my freeze-dried camping meals with canteen water for dinner.

Water would be a problem. I couldn't find any water source nearby, so I sparingly used what I had brought along and was glad I had arranged to be picked up in a few days.

When darkness came, I could see the fires of a small village on the far side of the bay. I assumed that meant that they could also see my fire. I tried to learn more of the local Creole language from the book I bought in Port-Au-Prince, but couldn't read very well by the light of my campfire, so decided it was time for bed.

As I lie in my hammock, I quickly realized it was going to be a long and uncomfortable night. The hammock bent my back in half just as it had done before. It also arched my head uncomfortably and had me sliding around the taut canvas bed. I got out and pulled a towel out from my pack and rolled it up as a pillow, but it also kept sliding away.

Then the drums started from across the bay, followed by hysterical screaming. A voodoo sacrifice? There were three drums. The first one had a high-pitched sound. This was later joined by one with a medium pitch, then a deep bass drum. A baby, mama and papa drum? I got out of the hammock and brought my machete inside. If I was going to be the sacrifice, I would give myself a fighting chance.

Then the pouring rain came. It was a mixed blessing.

I quickly scrambled out of the hammock and set up my cooking pot to catch rainwater. After dinner, I had washed it in seawater, so I first rinsed out the salt that had crusted on the bottom. Then I got back into my hammock for protection from the downpour.

I got another hammock lesson.

The wind blew the rain right through the mosquito netting. The tarp on top was not wide enough to keep it out. Fortunately, I was able to fix this by pulling down the netting and tucking it under my arms, which then pulled the tarp directly over me. It was a bit claustrophobic, but kept the rain out.

However, it was still a long night.

The next morning I woke up to a stark naked native standing just outside my hammock staring at me. He was holding a machete and a conch shell. I quickly unzipped my way out of the hammock. However, instead of reaching for my machete, I rummaged through my pack for the book *"Creole for English Speaking People."*

I'd start with diplomacy.

I quickly noted that he had a real machete, designed for cutting cane or jungle brush. It was shorter than mine, had a thick, sharp blade with a rounded end and a sizable wooden handle that offered a good grip. Perfect for hacking your way through the jungle. On the contrary, I still had the U.S. camping supplies store variety with a thin blade and a plastic handle that was too short and narrow to provide a good grip.

He was not being aggressive in any way, but just stood there and repeated the same words over and over again.

I scrambled through the dictionary, and after several minutes of barely understood exchanges back and forth, I realized he just wanted to sell me the conch, noting that the meat would make good eating. I should have bought it.

I didn't know how to make conch chowder, but the shell would be a good souvenir and story. In retrospect, I should have offered to buy his machete. That would have been a real prize. But I was not thinking very well on my feet, so lost the opportunity.

He took the refusal graciously, got into a dugout canoe and paddled back across the bay.

But thinking back to my Virgin Islands experience, I felt that once the locals try to sell you something that you don't want, it's best to move on. Especially now that they knew I was there.

Although I hadn't honed any jungle survival skills here, I felt that I had enough of a "jungle experience" to go home.

*Chapter Nine*

# The Search Begins

In 1997, Grammy was living with my mother in San Diego while I was living in Chicago, working for a global advertising agency.

Grammy had been forced to sell the home we grew up in with all its great memories and history due to advancing property taxes. The state showed no mercy, despite the fact that her husband volunteered as an ambulance driver in World War I, registered for the World War II draft at age 46 and she lost her only son in that war.

My mother agreed to take her in. The two never got along like most mothers and daughters and they made it awkward for me because they always tried to get me to take sides in their arguments.

Nevertheless, I tried to visit at least once a year. During one visit, Grammy said she wanted to show me something and took me into the dining room. There, she opened a drawer from a desk cabinet I recognized from her home in Maplewood. It was one of those desk and cabinet combinations that had drawers on the bottom but a flap on the top that pulled down and became a desktop which was supported by flat wooden spars that emerged when you pulled down the top. It contained some documents related to Larry's missing status in World War II as well as the letters he wrote home to his mother and sister.

"I want to see him before I die," Grammy said, presenting the documents. "Can you help me find him?"

"I will do my best," I replied. I had never seen these documents before and wasn't sure why she had never shown them to me in the past. Unfortunately, at this point, most people that knew him had already passed away. If Grammy had shared these documents just a few years earlier, it would have made a big difference. Similarly, my mother could have introduced me to people who knew him. Again, a few years difference was critical.

Before, the idea of searching for Larry had just been a fantasy. A magic carpet ride by an imaginative kid. Now it was a reality.

The first thing that caught my eye was a Western Union telegram dated March 10, 1944, 9.21 p.m. addressed to my grandmother. It read:

> THE SECRETARY OF WAR DESIRES ME TO EXPRESS HIS DEEP REGRET THAT YOUR SON STAFF SERGEANT LAWRENCE GRASHA HAS BEEN REPORTED MISSING SINCE ONE MARCH IN AMERICAN AREA PERIOD IF FURTHER DETAILS OR OTHER INFORMATION ARE RECEIVED YOU WILL BE PROMPTLY NOTIFIED PERIOD THE ADJUTANT GENERAL

Very cold, I thought. The telegram was followed by a letter dated March 12 confirming the details, but offering some hope. It noted that "missing" just means that his current whereabouts is not known and that experience has shown that many persons reported missing are subsequently reported as returned to duty or being hospitalized for injuries. It further noted that his pay, allowances and allotments would continue until his status was established. It was signed by J. A. Ulio, Major General, The Adjutant General.

On April 10, 1944, Grammy received a follow-up letter that read:

*Dear Mrs. Grasha:*

*Under date of March 10, 1944, The Adjutant General notified you that your son, Staff Sergeant Lawrence Grasha, had been reported missing in the American Area since March 1, 1944.*

*Further information has been received indicating that Sergeant Grasha was a crew member of a B-24, (Liberator) bomber which departed from Waller Field, Trinidad at about 6:09 a.m. local time at Trinidad on a ferrying mission to Belem, Brazil. Full details are not available, but the report indicates that your son's plane was last contacted by radio at about 8:23am at which time the plane, apparently in no difficulty, was flying over the Atlantic Ocean off the coast of Georgetown, British Guiana. When the Liberator failed to arrive at its destination an immediate search was instigated but, unfortunately, up to the present time neither the missing craft nor its crew members have been found. Inasmuch as there has been no further observation or contact with the plane there is, I regret to say, no other information available at the present time.*

*The great anxiety caused you by failure to receive more details concerning you son's disappearance is fully realized. Please be assured that any additional information received will be conveyed immediately to you by the Adjutant General or this headquarters.*

*Very sincerely,*
*T. A. Fitzpatrick,*
*Colonel, A. G. D.*

*Air Adjutant General*

The next telegram was even more blunt than the first. Dated May 27, 1944

> MRS MARY GRASHA
> 109 ORCHARD RD MAPLEWOOD NJ
> THE SECRETARY OF WAR ASKS THAT I ASSURE YOU OF HIS DEEP REGRET IN THE LOSS OF YOUR SON STAFF SERGEANT LAWRENCE GRASHA WHO WAS PREVIOUSLY REPORTED MISSING REPORTS RECEIVED IN THE WAR DEPARTMENT ESTABLISH THE FACT THAT YOUR SONS DEATH OCCURRED ON ONE MARCH IN THE AMERICAN AREA LETTER FOLLOWS=
> DUNLOP ACTING THE ADJUTANT GENERAL

The next letter, dated May 30, 1944, confirmed the telegram. It read:

*Dear Mrs. Grasha:*

*It is with profound regret that I confirm the recent telegram informing you of the death of your son, Staff Sergeant Lawrence Grasha 12,164,098, Air Corps, who was previously reported missing on 1 March 1944 in the American Area, while in flight to Belem, Brazil.*

*An official message has now been received which states that he was killed on the date he was previously reported missing. An extensive search by Naval Blimps and Army Aircraft failed to reveal any trace of your son.*

*If additional information is received it will be transmitted to you.*

*I realize the burden of anxiety that has been yours since he was first reported missing and deeply regret the sorrow this later report brings you. May the knowledge that he served his country bravely be of sustaining comfort to you.*

*My sympathy is with you in this time of great sorrow.*

*Sincerely yours,*
*ROBERT H. DUNLOP*
*Brigadier General,*
*Acting The Adjutant General*

However, Grammy was skeptical. What reports confirmed his death? If they had reports, why didn't they provide them? They said they had no trace of him, so why did they assume he was dead? Was it just a ruse to stop paying his salary?

Larry was nineteen years old at the time. Still a teenager. In four months, he would have just reached twenty.

Another document in the drawer indicated that Larry had taken out a $10,000 life insurance policy naming his family as beneficiaries. Apparently, all soldiers had this opportunity. If you guesstimate an annual interest rate of 3-4 percent, this would amount to anywhere from $84,000 to $168,000 in 2016 money. Not a small sum. However, the terms of the policy paid it out over Grammy's lifetime and not as a lump sum. In return for Larry's monthly contribution of $6.40, Grammy was guaranteed $45 a month for life. In 1990, the amount was raised to $78 a month.

*Chapter Ten*

# Congressmen

I wasn't sure how to begin my research, so I did what any American would typically do. I wrote to Grammy's congressman in California.

Well, I thought I did. My sister lived in California close to Grammy, so I asked her if she could get me the details. She said she would try.

However, she didn't try that hard, it seemed, because she gave me the name of the wrong congressman. I sent him a detailed letter early January 1997 and his staff quickly replied indicating that Grammy was not in his congressional district, but graciously said they would pass on my letter and documents to the correct congressman and gave me the contact details.

One month later, the correct congressman's staff provided me with several documents. Unfortunately, the repository of all military personnel files, the National Personnel Records Center in St. Louis, Missouri had experienced a fire in 1973 and many military personnel files were lost including those of Uncle Larry. At that time, they could only provide me with "partial" records which only gave his date of enlistment, date of birth and Army Air Corps Serial number.

However, from other sources, they supplied me with a key document titled "Missing Air Crew Report," which provided a summary of his departure location and destination as well as all the other crew members and a map of the airplane's flight route.

It advanced my search plans significantly.

They also provided another document that was from a database of hospital records during the period. It indicated that Larry had not appeared in any hospital and concluded that he was not found. The report used the words "not found" seven times.

*Chapter Eleven*
# Missing Air Crew

The Missing Air Crew Report provided details of Larry's last flight, but it omitted other key information.

The MACR indicated that aircraft B-24-H with serial number 41-28773 departed from Waller Field on March 1, 1943 at 1009Z. I knew from my ham radio days as a teenager that the "Z" stood for "Zulu time", radio operator slang for GMT or Greenwich Mean Time. That would have been 06.09 a.m. Trinidad time.

The estimated time of arrival in Belém, Brazil was 1709Z, so a seven hour flight. That meant the B-24's average cruising speed was 160 mph. The weather was generally good, but had light showers and the plane flew for 30 minutes on instruments.

According to the MACR, the last radio report was abeam of Georgetown, British Guiana, about 60 miles offshore. The plane was on a southeast heading towards the northeast coast of South America and Paramaribo, Dutch Guiana. From there, it would continue on the same heading, overflying French Guiana then onwards to Brazil.

British Guiana and Dutch Guiana were the colonial names of what later became the independent countries of Guyana and Suriname while French Guiana remained an overseas outpost of France. During World War II it ultimately decided not to support the Vichy government established by Germany after its invasion of France and fortunately teamed up with the Allies. Otherwise, it would have been a good stepping stone for the German military with designs on the U.S. and the Caribbean, especially U-boats. Of course, if it hadn't the Allies could have easily captured it. Another French possession in the Caribbean, Martinique, remained with Vichy France until mid-1943. But after the U.S. planned an invasion while implementing several blockades, Martinique made the smart choice and sided with the Allies.

There were three designated air routes from Waller Field to Belém. Two were non-stop and the other one made stops in Georgetown and Paramaribo, also known as "Para." I'm guessing that the two-stop route was primarily for fighters that didn't have the range to fly non-stop to Belém. Also, a number of fighters reportedly went down around Paramaribo.

In fact, there were two Missing Air Crew Reports, an initial one prepared on March 1, 1944 by E. A. Bradunas, Lt. Col., AC and F. W. Muench, Capt, AC and another one signed by an unnamed base operations officer with the rank of major and an unintelligible signature on March 3, 1944.

Both reports indicated that the aircraft was attached to Project #AQ7, but indicated no Squadron, Group or Detachment. The initial report indicated that there might have been a fire on board, because a number of planes had been delayed by fuel leaks over the previous three weeks. But that was pure speculation by the ground crew.

Even if there were a fire, the crew would have time to radio that event to one of several stations along the coast. Also, in case of an emergency and bailout, radio operators were instructed to lock down their Morse code key so it transmitted a continuous signal that could be tracked. There was a lever on the side of the key that easily let you do that. In fact, that's the first thing you did when tuning your transmitter. Even if there was an explosion, they were so close to the coast that someone would have heard it.

Another theory was that the plane might have been shot down by a German submarine. The South Atlantic and Caribbean was still a back door for German submarines to America but less so in 1944.

Fortunately, Germany archived very meticulous records of its submarine activity and none reported shooting down an American bomber on the day Larry's aircraft disappeared. However, 1944 was a very bad year for the German undersea craft. Reportedly 249 U-boats were lost that year. In 1943, the Germans lost a reported 244 U-boats. Maybe Uncle Larry had something to do with it.

The supplement to the MACR provided the serial numbers of the plane's engines as well as the full name of the crew and their serial numbers. There were six airmen on board and two passengers:

1st Lt. James S. Buchanan, Pilot, 0-445417

2nd Lt. Victor R. Harmon, Co-Pilot, 0-691499

2nd Lt. John F. Healy, Navigator, 0-741262

Staff Sgt. Eldon D. Hunter Jr., Engineer, 34386241

Staff Sgt. Lawrence Grasha, Radio Operator, 12164098

Sgt. Don L. Maheno, Gunner, 34198994

Cpl. Benjamin M. Evans, Radar Mechanic, 32675202

Cpl. Louis J. Enderle, Radar Mechanic, 36281580

The radar mechanics were designated as passengers and all onboard, except Evans, had the letters "DED" hand written next to their names, which I took to mean deceased. The letters "DNB" were written next to Evans.

A WWII researcher I later communicated with found that very strange. He said that DNB meant "dead not buried" and suggested that all the bodies were accounted for except Evans. Others suggested that this was just a sloppy administrative mistake.

He also found it strange that the mission was described simply as "ferry," whereas other documents indicated that the plane was flown by a combat crew. Did that mean that they were ferrying the aircraft and cargo and crew to a war zone or just dropping off a plane? If so, what was the cargo? It was not indicated. Also why was their group, squadron or detachment not defined and what was Project or Organization AQ7 or AQ7A?

Before Larry left the U.S. he sent his family a forwarding address postcard with an APO address. APO stood for "Army Post Office," a military post office box with a U.S. address. The mail would be sent on to the addressee. Larry indicated his APO as Project FM-070-AQ7A. However, someone had subsequently crossed that out and wrote in APO 2806, New York, NY. I know Larry didn't write that in because his plane went missing March 1 and the card was postmarked March 2, Langley Field after he had already departed and was declared missing. However, APO 2806 doesn't appear in the directory of WWII APOs. The handwriting was not clear and it could have been APO 7806 but that number also does not exist in the records.

Meanwhile, I knew that "FM" in army speak could mean "field manual" because camping stores were selling the army field manual for "Survival, Evasion and Escape, which I bought and brought along to the Virgin Islands with me.

77

Research indicated that FM-070 could have been a manual teaching pilots how to identify, evade or engage Italian warplanes.

But to date, the U.S. Department of Defense can not or will not tell me what was Organization AQ7 or identify location of the APO number.

*Chapter Twelve*
# B-24 Liberator Bomber

The B-24 was designed as a long-range strategic heavy bomber. The brief from the U.S. government to potential bidders on the project was to produce an aircraft that could fly further, faster and carry more payload than the existing B-17 bomber first manufactured by the Boeing Airplane Company.

The B-17 bomber was popularly known as "The Flying Fortress" because of all the gun turrets it carried. The "B" was a military designation that indicated the aircraft as a bomber and not Boeing as the manufacturer. All military aircraft had such designations. For example, in the Army Air Forces, "P" stood for pursuit aircraft such as the famous P-40 fighters that made up the "Flying Tigers" unit in China.

The contract for the B-24 was won by the Consolidated Aircraft Corporation of San Diego, California, but they later licensed production to the Ford Motor Company and the Douglas Aircraft Company.

While the B-17 was widely known as the "Flying Fortress," the B-24 was referred to as the "Liberator." Its detractors also referred to it as the "Flying Boxcar" due to its heavy flat-sided fuselage and square nose. Others referred to it as the "Flying Coffin" because of its cramped interior and the difficulty of bailing out in an emergency, especially for turret ball gunners.

In this regard, there was friendly competition between B-17 and B-24 crews over who flew the best and prettiest airplane. The B-17 had a rounded nose and a sleek fuselage whereas the B-24 had a flat, box-like nose, slab sides and twin tails that gave it a more clunky, square-like appearance. Allegedly, Consolidated even did market research among the general public to gauge their awareness and opinions of the aircraft. Some wondered how something as big and heavy as the Liberator could even get off the ground.

Meanwhile, I couldn't find consistent specs on the aircraft.

Both aircraft had four engines and both served throughout all theaters of World War II. According to one source, the B-24 had a wingspan of 110 feet and was 67 feet long. It was powered by four 1,200 horsepower engines which gave it a maximum speed of 290mph, a range of 3,000 miles, and a service ceiling of 28,000 feet. It was armed with ten .50 caliber machine guns and manned by a crew of ten, consisting of four officers and six enlisted men.

Some sources indicated that it could fly up to 40,000 feet, though it typically operated between 10,000 and 20,000 feet at a cruising speed of 160 mph so the crew wouldn't have to use oxygen. Other sources indicated its cruising speed closer to 200 mph.

Consolidated constantly made improvements to the aircraft based on field tests and combat experience and the B-24-A model was quickly supplanted by models, B, C, D, E, F, G, H and more. Reportedly, it could take a lot of punishment and still make it home, even full of holes and with half its rudders blown off.

The news reels we see of the innocent black puffs of flak don't reveal the hundreds of shards of shrapnel they released when exploded which easily punctured the light aluminum skin of the aircraft and crippled its engines or slashed its crew to pieces. Flak was like aerial hand grenades but significantly more powerful. Planes returning from bombing missions were often littered with body parts throughout the fuselage. Reportedly the word "flak" was an acronym based on the German word *Fliegerabwehrkanone,* which translated as "aircraft defense cannon."

According to the Aircraft Record Card, Uncle Larry's B-24 was built by Douglas Aircraft Company in Tulsa, Oklahoma and designated as model B-24-H-15. The number fifteen at the end was a bit of a mystery. It was also referred to as HYBRID in various reports. Was this just a radio call sign or an indication that their plane had been modified to carry and operate some advanced technology?

It was delivered to Langley Field, Virginia January 25, 1944. Larry had been stationed there since August 1943 and had previously been flying in B-17s according to his girlfriend.

However, the Aircraft Record Card also indicated that the plane's last station was Presque Isle, Maine and it had departed the U.S. on February 8. The pilot's military records indicate that he was posted to Langley Field, but that his last posting was Presque Isle, Maine. This would have suggested a flight to Europe. Yet he was also declared missing on the Trinidad to Brazil flight as cited in the Missing Air Crew report.

Since the pilot had previously been stationed at Langley Field, my only conclusion is that he was sent up to Maine to procure the aircraft, then fly it down to Langley Field to pick up the rest of the crew for their flight to South America.

Again, the bizarre thing about Uncle Larry's Missing Aircrew Report was that it claimed they were attached to Project #AQ7.

On the other hand, the pilot's file indicated he was attached to "Organization" AQ7, but assigned to Project 90434R, as were the rest of the crew including Larry.

It sounded like they were seconded to some secret handshake organization and I have yet to find out anything about it.

The Aircraft record card also indicated that the plane was bound for ELM8. There was no such destination listed in the records. But ELMS would have been Algeria, so maybe this was just a typo.

I tried to find pilots who flew the aircraft, hopefully those who flew the South Atlantic route and found an association called The International B-24 Liberator Club which published a quarterly news bulletin. Ironically, it was located just down the street from where my mother and grandmother lived in San Diego. I posted an ad in the bulletin looking for pilots as well as anyone who may have known Larry.

There were many ads from other people looking for lost relatives, indicating the trauma of losing a loved one without knowing the cause.

I found one former pilot who was living in Florida and claimed he had flown the South Atlantic route to Brazil. It was a tough conversation because he was over ninety years old, hard of hearing and I needed to shout into the telephone to make myself heard.

He said it was a very dangerous route despite what pilots were told in the briefing room. He claimed that the pilots were assured that they'd be close to the coast and have access to radio stations along the way. However, he said that it was terrifying to fly over the ocean because no pilot would want to ditch a B-24 in the water and the plane was known for mechanical failures so you might be forced to do it.

He explained that as soon as the plane belly-flopped into the sea, the force of impact would rip the bomb bay doors open, water would rush in and split the fuselage in half. He noted that the survival rate of an emergency water landing was very low. He claimed that the crew had less than ten seconds to escape the aircraft before they were trapped inside and drowned. However, as the plane broke up in the water, it would still be skipping along the sea from its forward momentum so it was every man for himself.

However, if they bailed out over the ocean they would likely be scattered all over the sea, lose contact with each other, be hard to spot and probably die from exposure. Meanwhile, in less than an hour, the airplane would sink like a stone.

One source indicated that the crew survival rate of a B-24 ditching in the ocean was less than thirty percent.

At the same time, he indicated that it was terrifying to fly over the jungle, because if you had a problem, there was no place to land. And if you had to bail out over the dense jungle, you'd be caught in the two hundred foot canopy of the tropical rainforest and either die falling to the ground from a collapsed parachute or trying to climb down from the tree tops.

"But it was war," he noted. "We just did it and didn't think about it."

Of the three designated routes to Belém, only one followed the coast. The other two overflew the jungles of Suriname and French Guiana. Since they were flying to Belém, a coastal town just past the Amazon River. I didn't understand why all routes didn't just follow the coast.

If you crashed in the water, you had a small chance of survival, but if you crashed in the jungle, you had almost zero chance of survival. Not even ten seconds worth.

## Chapter Thirteen
# Radar

Radar was one of the more important technologies developed early in World War II.

It allowed Britain to spot German bombers miles before they reached the coast and scramble their fighter planes to intercept them. Similarly, it could have given the U.S. a jump on the Japanese planes about to attack Pearl Harbor, but the data was dismissed by commanders and attributed to a fleet of returning U.S. aircraft.

Like all data, it's only as good as the person interpreting it. Otherwise, it's garbage in, garbage out as they say.

From the Missing Aircrew Report, I noted that there were two radar technicians onboard. I didn't really think anything of it at the time. I assumed they were part of the normal crew and operated the aircraft's radar.

I found out about Langley Field's connection to radar only later in my research.

As previously noted, Langley Field was primarily charged with scouring the U.S. East Coast for German submarines. However, once the U-boat threat abated it focused on various advanced technologies. Primarily radar. For example, radar that could "see" through the clouds and bad weather so the bombardier did not have to physically sight the target. The radar would paint a picture of it. Also, long range navigational radar that most boaters took for granted before GPS called LORAN.

LORAN, an acronym for long range navigation had stations around the world that sent out coded signals. When you turned on the LORAN receiver on your boat, you got two numbers. You compared them to lines on the chart and the intersection of the lines indicated where you were within maybe ten miles.

The high altitude radar, known as H2X meant that the bombers could fly higher and be less vulnerable to flak and fighters, though the crew would be placed under severe strain due to the extreme cold and the need to use unreliable oxygen systems at the bone-chilling altitudes. If the crew were required to pull on oxygen masks, they often froze up or fogged up and their sheep's wool flight suits were not sufficient to keep them warm especially with the airflow coming through the waist-gun window. If they took off their gloves to touch their guns or equipment, their skin stuck to the metal. Going to the toilet was unheard of in those conditions and the crew often just pissed in their pants.

But allegedly this radar system was so sophisticated that it was used right up through the Vietnam War.

The other technology was called MAD. This was before the atomic bomb so the mnemonic of "mutually assured destruction" later associated with that acronym did not apply.

In this instance MAD referred to a Magnetic Anomaly Detector. This was a technology that recognized disturbances in the earth's magnetic field. That meant airplanes could detect enemy submarines underwater. Ironically, it was developed at my alma matter, Columbia University.

However, if you believe some of the scary stories about MAD, it sent out a powerful electromagnetic beam that could also affect the behavior and perceptions of humans, even causing them to hallucinate. Humans are bio-electro-magnetic entities. And I've read press reports about mental disturbances in people living close to power stations because of the magnetic fields they generated.

The science fiction writers took it one step further. They referenced something called the "Philadelphia Experiment," in which a docked ship with crew on board was wrapped with giant cables and a huge current sent through the wires to generate a mega magnetic field. The scientists called it "degaussing" and it was supposed to make the ship invisible to enemy radar.

However, according to the various stories, the testing procedure made the ship invisible to observers on shore and when they turned off the current, they found that some of the crew had their bodies physically melded with the ship while others claimed they traveled in time. Of course, the U.S. government dismissed the reporting of the incident as a hoax.

Much of this research was conducted by physicists at MIT, Bell Labs and Columbia University where I went to school. According to his letters, Larry spent some time during this period "going back to school" but he didn't specify where.

My mother once told me that Larry was involved in a "secret project" but I wrote this off as the boasting of a frustrated soldier on the home front trying to impress his sister or my mother trying to impress me.

As I was digging into this on the Internet, I stumbled into a website by some filmmakers in Newfoundland, Canada who were doing a documentary about the commander of Larry's airbase, Langley Field, Colonel William C. Dolan.

Apparently, he was in a B-24 bomber carrying some super advanced technology that was supposed to bring a quick end to the war, but the plane crashed in Newfoundland during a snowstorm on its way to England.

I immediately contacted the filmmakers.

They were incredibly savvy researchers and quickly associated AQ7 with an advanced radar system although they couldn't identify it specifically. They also felt it was more than a coincidence that both planes carrying similar equipment crashed or went missing.

Something was not quite right.

Larry's plane was forced to take off although the pilot felt there was a problem with the engines and wanted to delay the flight. Separately, his commander's plane was forced to fly through bad weather and crashed on its way to Newfoundland before it reached Europe.

Could there have been a mole or German sympathizer in the system who made sure this technology never made its way to the front lines?

*Chapter Fourteen*
# Initial Plans

As noted, according to the Missing Air Crew Report, the plane's last radio report was off the coast of Georgetown, British Guiana.

The documents further indicated that the pilot was required to report in over Zandery Field in Suriname, then again over Rochambeau Field in French Guiana. The documents did not indicate any further communication after British Guiana, however, the radio logs and communication texts were missing from the file.

Interestingly, the person in charge of these files said they would not be able to locate them because I couldn't provide his unit name and Organization AQ7 was not a recognized unit.

So my initial assumption was that the plane went down in the sea before reaching Suriname. I was a certified bareboat sailing captain and scuba diver so I knew a little about the sea. I immediately got the navigational charts for that area.

The charts indicated that the plane's last reported radio position was only over water about 150 feet deep and it was heading toward land where the depth would quickly drop to sixty then thirty feet. So, my first reaction was that this could be an easy scuba search. At that depth you could stay down for at least an hour without any need for decompression procedures. It would be a very safe dive.

I started to research and plan a sea search.

*Chapter Fifteen*
# Ted Kaufman

Needless to say, I was telling all my friends about this project, hoping to get ideas and leads.

One interested friend was a colleague from university who gave horseback riding lessons to some of the rich and famous at his girlfriend's stables north of New York City.

After hearing my story, he introduced me to Ted Kaufman. Kaufman was a dowser. A dowser was someone who found water by wandering around a field holding a forked stick. When the stick pointed downward, there was supposed to be water there. As a child I was shown this technique by Grammy's brother on his farm during one visit. He called it a diving rod and used it to dig wells.

However, Kaufman was much more sophisticated than that and didn't just find water. In fact, he was retained by U.S. law enforcement agencies to find missing persons and criminals hiding out or on the run.

His technique involved swinging a pendulum over a map, then honing in on a location with a ruler based on the pendulum direction. He'd move a ruler vertically with a swinging pendulum over it until he felt he got a strong "signal" and drew a line across it. Then he'd repeat the process moving the ruler horizontally. The intersection of the two lines would be the location.

One of his most famous cases involved finding two men who disappeared one night in the Lake George area of upstate New York.

The men went out one night in their pickup truck to buy some groceries but never returned. The local police were stumped. As a last desperate measure, they approached Ted Kaufman.

He performed his technique in front of them and his lines intersected in the middle of Lake George, a huge inland lake about thirty-five miles long and several miles wide. The police were skeptical and let it go. However, sometime later, they decided to investigate the spot, and asked Ted to come aboard their police boat and dowse the area as they were underway. He arrived with a forked stick and directed the boat to a spot based on the signals he got from his diving rod.

When he told the boat to stop, they dropped an anchor and it actually bounced off the the truck bed. Divers went down and confirmed the truck was there.

They theorized that the driver thought he could take a short cut home by driving across the frozen lake, but the ice was too thin and the truck fell through and they drowned in the icy waters.

I spoke with Ted over the phone and he was very candid about my case.

"You know, so much time has passed," he noted. "I'm not sure I can help you. But I'd be willing to give it a shot."

"What is your fee?" I asked.

"Well, if I don't feel good about it, I won't charge you anything," he replied.

"And if you do feel good about?" I continued somewhat cynically.

"Well, if I do feel good about it, I'd ask you to make a small donation to my association. I believe this is a technique that can be learned, and I am training others to do it," he replied.

"So, what would be a small donation?" I asked again somewhat cynically.

"Twenty dollars would be fine," he replied.

I ultimately gave him one hundred.

I asked him what he needed to proceed and he indicated he needed a picture of Larry, his plane and a map of the area.

I told him I didn't have a picture of the actual plane, but could provide a picture of the type of plane. He replied that would be fine. I also gave him a very broad map covering North and South America. I wanted to test his methodology and didn't want to reveal too much information. The only specifics I offered were that the plane was flying from Florida to Brazil and lost somewhere in between.

After a week, Kaufman called me on the phone. He wanted to know if I could get him a large-scale map of French Guiana. He thought he found something there, but wanted to be sure.

Fortunately, the travel bookstore and map supplier, Rand McNally, was still in business in Chicago on Michigan Avenue and stocked maps for the most exotic destinations in the world. And who knows why, but they had maps of French Guiana. I bought two and sent one to Kaufman.

A week later, he claimed that he had a fix on my uncle's airplane, but was especially surprised because he felt it was a very strong fix. He didn't believe it himself. So he gave the map to one of his colleagues who also got a strong fix within less than one mile of Kaufman's. I named Ted's fix as "X" and his colleague's fix as "X Prime," or X' which was nomenclature I picked up in high school math class.

The coordinates for X were:

Latitude North 3 degrees 57.3 minutes. Longitude West 52 degrees 45.5 minutes.

The coordinates for X' were:

Latitude North 3 degrees 57.3 minutes. Longitude West 52 degrees 45.65 minutes.

Longitude and Latitude are not comparable measures. Longitude represents the lines on the globe going north and south, while latitude represents the lines going east and west. The difference is that lines of latitude are parallel so measure the same distance anywhere on the globe. However, the lines of longitude converge at the poles, so the distances get smaller as you go north or south.

Bottom line X and X' were less than a mile apart.

So, the plan was to get to X then head for X', surveying the area along the way.

Meanwhile, I called a friend in Paris who contacted the French agency that produced the French Guiana maps and they were willing to provide the actual aerial photos they used to make them. They apologized, noting that the photos were from the 1950s, but I thought that was even better because they were closer to the date of the airplane's disappearance. Additionally, they could provide me with topographic maps of the country.

Several things really grabbed my attention.

First, Kaufman's X on the map was within a mile or so of the plane's projected flight path. I hadn't given Ted Kaufman this information and there was no way he could have known it in advance.

Second, one of the images I got from the aerial photographs that the French agency had used to make the map showed an airplane-like profile in the same area. I enlarged it fifty times and it definitely looked like an airplane fuselage.

It was near a mountain called *Pic du Croissant*, presumably named after the French pastry that the mountain's shape resembled. According to the aerial photo, there was also a long barren clearing along the mountain that looked like someone had hacked out a small airstrip.

I ordered additional prints of the film to double check, but this time the image of the airplane fuselage was not there. The French mapping agency explained it must have been a piece of dust on the negative when they processed it. But I was not convinced.

A speck of dust looks like a dot on the film, not an airplane fuselage.

*Chapter Sixteen*

# New Plans

Based on the research from Kaufman, I started re-planning.

It seemed a lot easier to explore a jungle location than conduct an underwater search and I started developing contacts in French Guiana. It was a mystical option, but Ted had an impressive track record. I had no expectations and treated it as a testable hypothesis.

So I started looking for a helicopter pilot in Cayenne, the capital of French Guiana who could take me to the location, wait for me while I scouted around, then bring me back to the city.

It seemed pretty straightforward.

Of course, my first thought was to call the U.S. Embassy there, but they weren't very helpful and not interested. So I went back to Rand McNally's bookstore in Chicago, found a South American guidebook that included a section on French Guiana and started calling up hotels asking for helicopter pilot referrals.

I quickly realized that there were going to be language barriers. French versus English.

I had studied French for two years in university. However, American schools never really taught you a foreign language. You learned a lot of vocabulary and grammar and completed many translations, but you still couldn't communicate with the average person on the street.

So I enrolled in Berlitz. I can't say it was a better solution. The entire class was in French and they refused to explain anything in English, even nuances of grammar. Trying to understand a point of grammar in French could take two one-hour lessons, when they could make it clear in English in five minutes. Maybe that was part of their business strategy. At least I could buy French grammar books in English to help me out.

Meanwhile, one hotel in French Guiana came through for me. The Novotel. It was a French international chain. Their staff spoke English and were very supportive of my mission. I was very direct. I explained my project and asked them if they could help me find a helicopter pilot.

They introduced me to Michele Vanderbecq. The hotel claimed that Michele regularly supplied helicopters and guides into the rainforest, primarily for mining and logging companies.

I made the call.

Fortunately, Michele spoke English. I told her the story of my search and asked if she could help me find a pilot. I felt like I was in a *Star Wars* movie looking for a rogue adventurer to fly me to a secret galaxy. She seemed interested not just professionally but personally. She told me to call her back in a week.

"I found you a pilot," she explained. "But it may not be that easy."

"Why is that?" I asked.

"There may be no place to land in that area," she replied.

"Can he drop me down on a wire?" I asked, somewhat naively.

"No. Because the trees are two hundred feet high and if the wire gets caught in them, he needs to let it go and you will die. Otherwise, it will pull him into the trees and he will die.

"He needs to find a place to land and it may not be too close, so you need a guide to go with you."

"Ok. How much for him to find a place to land?" I asked.

"Don't worry," she responded. "He flies over that area a lot and said he will look for a place on one of his trips. You don't need to pay. He respects your story."

"Ok. When he finds the landing spot, send me the coordinates, so I can plan the trip," I responded. "And what about the guide."

"I already have one for you. He is very good. You can trust him. His name is Stephane. He walked across the entire country by himself through the jungle. He is our Indiana Jones."

I was sold.

Michele had her own interesting story. She and her husband had come from France to the Caribbean many years earlier to set up an import/export company. Michelle had spent time with most of the French communities around the region and could tell you about all of them on any of the islands. She had most recently come from Guadeloupe, but ended up in French Guiana for better opportunities.

"The island business is very small," she explained. "You need to be on the mainland."

While her husband focused on the trading business, she decided to promote jungle tourism and set up a company to do so. She already had a team of guides she could tap into and saw an opportunity for tourists from France looking for a unique tropical experience. Importantly, she commanded a roster of very serious, experienced jungle guides.

After a week, she sent me a fax indicating that the pilot had found a place a few miles from the Kaufman spot where he said we could land. So, I assumed that it would be a fairly easy hike. I called her on the phone to confirm.

"Are you sure the pilot can land there?" I asked.

"Yes. He already landed there as a test," she replied. "He is okay with it."

I later learned the hard way that walking a few miles in the jungle is not the same as walking a few miles through the park or even up and down the stairs of your apartment building.

"Thank you Michele," I responded. "Let's fix the date and I will make my plans."

"Ok, but the guide says you need to come during the good weather," she explained. "You need to come at the end of the rainy season so there will be water in the streams to drink. If you come too soon, the rain will be too much. But if you come too much later, you will have nothing to drink. It will be too heavy for you to carry your water."

"Ok. Give me some dates."

I called her a week later to confirm.

"The guide says it would be best for you to come in July," she explained. "He also says it would be best if you went into the jungle during a full moon because it will not be raining so much."

She gave me some dates and I made my plans to come in July, which ironically happened to be the month of Larry's birthday though I didn't know it at the time.

I called a week later to re-confirm.

"It is confirmed," she responded. "But there is a small problem. The place you want to go to in the country is a closed area. Nobody is allowed to go there because of many problems. There has been some smuggling and guerrillas in that area and they also want to protect it from mining.

"But don't worry. I already discussed it with the government and they will let you go for humanitarian reasons, but you must take one of their people along. You don't have to pay him, but he needs to go. He is very experienced. He worked with the French Foreign Legion here and it is always better to have more people along in case you have a problem."

His name was Pierre.

Apparently, Pierre was a scientist and spent time in jungles and deserts all over the world studying the wildlife and whatever. He was never a soldier in the Legion, but was an advisor for their jungle survival course in French Guiana.

"Ok. No problem," I replied. "Let's do it."

*Chapter Seventeen*
# Psychic Warning

I was still working in Chicago as I continued to plan my trip.

Meanwhile, my girlfriend there told me about this cool black-tie party at the Field Museum of Natural History. Various Chicago associations threw great events at notable landmarks, which they turned into stunning black-tie party venues. This one was on the top of the list.

But we heard about it late and were not on the list. Being the eager-to-please boyfriend I was at that time, I suggested that I show up early to see if I could get tickets then call her if I could. Easier for a guy to throw on a tuxedo and bow tie than for a lady to make herself up. I promised that if I couldn't get us in, we'd go somewhere special for dinner that night.

As luck would have it, I got in. Because it was still very early, there was not a lot going on except a bunch of girls lined up in front of several "psychics" who were hired to provide entertainment for the evening.

I grabbed myself a Heineken from the bar, then strolled over for a closer look. I called my girlfriend, who said she needed another half an hour, so I got in line to pass the time.

There were three so-called psychics.

One was dressed as a gypsy with a crystal ball, another as a wizard sporting robes and a pointed hat full of moons and stars. The third looked pretty bored with the whole affair. Ethnically, he appeared to be American Indian based on his dark complexion, long, braided locks kept in place with a head band, and a wooden stick chest vest.

That's the one I wanted. If anyone was in touch with the Great Spirit, it would be an American Indian.

The line before him was all women.

They asked typical girlie questions. All about boyfriends.

"Does he really love me or is he just using me for sex?"

"He smiled at my girlfriend. Are they having sex?"

"Is he serious about marrying me or just in it for the sex?"

When my turn came, I put down the Heineken and noted, "My question is a bit different."

The Indian looked up at me impassively.

"My uncle died in an airplane crash during World War II. Can you tell me where the airplane is?"

"I only read the cards," he replied. "Ten dollars."

"Shit," I said to myself. This guy is only a Tarot card reader. What a bunch of bullshit I thought silently, but plunked down a ten dollar note.

He had me shuffle the cards, cut the deck, then turn up a few cards off the top.

"Do it again," he replied after I went through the exercise.

I shuffled the deck, broke it in half, and turned up some more cards.

"Do it one more time," he instructed.

"Look, you can keep the ten dollars if it's not working. He's been dead a long time, so I understand."

"Just do it one more time," he replied, shooting me an ominous look.

I did it one more time and spread out another set of cards.

He nodded knowingly.

"The reason I asked you to do it three times," he explained. "Is because you said your uncle is dead. But each time the cards said he is alive. In fact you produced the strongest life cards in the deck. Three times in a row."

"If he's still alive, why didn't he come home?" I persisted. "He loved his family and wrote them every week. He would have crawled home to see them again."

"Cut the cards," the Indian instructed.

I played along and he made another pronouncement.

"It's very simple," the Indian explained. "He doesn't want to come home. He is ashamed to come home. He was crippled in the accident, maybe had his dick cut off and can't face his family. According to the cards, he had a fiancée. Is that correct?"

"Yes," I answered.

"So that's the story," he replied.

I persisted.

"Can you tell me where he is, or at least where the airplane is?"

In the meantime, I tried to empty my mind. I didn't believe in Tarot cards, but believed that someone could read your mind and play it back to you.

"It's not where you'd expect for World War II. It's not in Europe, Asia or Africa," he responded.

"I can only describe it," he continued. "It's a bad place. A jungle. It's full of gold, guns, mercenaries and smugglers. And they're tearing down the jungle to get to the gold."

He perfectly described everything I learned about French Guiana.

It had huge lodes of gold that were being extracted. And the French Legionnaires were essentially mercenaries. They were foreigners who had signed up to fight the overseas wars France didn't want to sacrifice its regular troops on, mostly in the backwaters of Africa. A successful tour of duty granted you a French passport. So if you survived the enlistment period, it was a good deal for Third World hopefuls or renegades evading the law or local politics. It gave someone a fresh start in life. A new name and country. Not to mention French food and culture.

It was a good deal for France and a good deal for Legionnaire volunteers.

On the contrary, one cynical French friend explained, "Nobody cares if we send in the Legion to these places," he explained to me. "Because they are not French. Only foreign mercenaries. So it causes no political problems."

However, when the French sent troops into Beirut, Lebanon when I was there as a journalist during the civil war in the 1980s, they not only sent in the Legion but regular troops. The Legion was not sent in to be cannon fodder but as highly trained special forces.

No other European country matched France's commitment to Lebanon at that time except Italy.

I continued my dialogue with the psychic.

"And what if I went to this place. Will I find him?" I asked.

"Cut the cards," came the reply.

I cut the cards.

"He doesn't want to be found. And if you go, you might find something you don't want to find," he noted.

"Wait," I protested. "Here's another ten dollars. I want to know more."

"I don't want your money," the Indian replied. "I don't want to tell you any more and I don't want to know any more. It's too intense. I can't explain it. There are powerful forces at work. You may die and others may die with you. I may die if I tell you anymore."

I retreated to the bar, grabbed another Heineken just as my girlfriend showed up. There was so much I wanted to tell her, but knew I couldn't tell her anything. I hoped that just holding her tightly in a slow dance would make it all right.

She sensed something was wrong and wanted to talk about it, but I felt that by telling her the story, she would become vulnerable to the evil forces at work.

We made the party rounds of everyone we knew and some that we didn't. But she noted that I was very distracted throughout the entire affair.

"Peter," she interrupted, "I think we should go."

"Ok," I replied without protest.

I got my car from the valet and we drove back to my place.

We undressed each other as soon as we got back to my apartment and made love. But it didn't still my brain or give me any comfort. I felt detached from the entire experience and she continued to sense that something was wrong.

"That wasn't making love," she noted. "That was only sex."

"Is this about us?" she asked from between the sheets.

I was still lost in my thoughts and barely acknowledged her.

"Us? What about us?" I responded.

"Is this about us?" she asked more forcefully.

"No. Not about us," I replied meekly. "It's about me. Something I need to do."

"I should go," she abruptly announced, got dressed and left.

I scarcely noticed.

*Chapter Eighteen*

# Spooked

While all this was going on, my sister called to tell me that Grammy was going into the hospital to remove a blockage in her intestines. Given her ninety-plus age, she might not survive the surgery, my sister indicated.

I was in Chicago and Grammy was in San Diego. I immediately dropped everything and caught the next flight out for what I thought might be the last time I would see her.

I entered Grammy's room at the hospital about five in the morning just before they were going to prep her for surgery. She was sleeping upright in a chair. This was not unusual because she was uncomfortable sleeping in a bed.

The sun was just coming up. The hospital told me that they needed to "put her under" by six a.m. so I should keep my conversation "short."

I patiently sat in a chair across the room and watched her, not sure what I might say when she woke up.

When she did wake up, her first words were, "Petey. I've been praying you'd be here.

"What about Larry?" she asked. "Did you find him?"

Those first words were unsettling, because I knew she was counting on me to solve his mystery before she died.

"I'm still doing research, Grammy," I replied. "But I have to ask you an important question.

"You are about to go in for some major surgery. I am going to wait for you and expect to see you on the other side. So you need to forget about Larry right now and focus all your energy on getting through this operation and seeing me on the other side. I will be waiting for you. You need to focus on that. I love you. You better be there. If you love me too, you will be there.

"Look, what if Larry walked into the room right now? What would it mean? So much time has passed. He wouldn't recognize you, you wouldn't recognize him. What would you talk about?"

Grammy quickly replied in a soft, sweet, loving tone, "Oh, if he walked in the room right now, I know I would faint, I'd be so happy to see him."

Then her tone switched into something very aggressive, a voice I never heard before, almost exorcist-like, and her face exuded sharp, dagger-like eyes that pinned me to the back of my seat.

"But then I'd pull myself back up on my feet and tell anyone who saw him or spoke to him that enough is enough. When you find him, you tell him that I don't care if he's injured or crippled or whatever. You tell him that I'm his mother and I love him, and I will take care of him, because that's what a mother's supposed to do!"

A chill ran down my spine.

She knew something. The American Indian psychic knew something.

They both knew some secret, but they couldn't tell me.

I didn't tell Grammy that I was off to the jungle in a few weeks. The last thing she needed to hear was about another "son" lost in the jungle.

Grammy seemed to know something that she couldn't share. My mother seemed to know something she couldn't share. But they both seemed sworn to silence. Maybe FBI agents showed up at their house and made them sign some secret document regarding Organization AQ7.

Or was it the insurance money? Did Larry call them two years after he went missing to tell his family that he was still alive, only to be told that they already cashed in his life insurance policy? I could easily see my mother having that conversation with him. But if Grammy knew, she would have given up everything to have him back home. And, as noted, the monthly payout was nothing.

Grammy survived the operation and was so pleased to see me waiting for her that she started kicking up the sheets in her bed. Sadly, I was the only family member there to greet here.

The doctors explained that they had removed a lump from her intestines, but she now needed to wear a bag on her stomach to catch all her body waste.

"I can't live like this, Petey," she said, noting the bag.

They said that she could have another operation to reattach her intestines but it was risky and they wanted her to recover from the first operation before performing a second one.

I assumed everything was under control.

It was not.

Some weeks later, I got a call from my sister indicating that "Grammy is not doing too well" and would urgently need another operation.

Instead of jumping on the next flight to California, I did the corporately responsible thing. I booked the red-eye flight and spent the day, getting all my projects updated with my staff and clients.

I was too late. She died while I was in flight. I felt it halfway there. A feeling of loss suddenly came over me. I knew it was Grammy.

Nobody blamed me for it, but I blamed myself. My presence somehow gave her energy, and if I had been there, she'd still be alive, I believed.

On the other hand, my friends were pretty practical about it.

"Well, now you don't need to go to French Guiana," they said.

"No. I made a promise to find her son," I replied. "And now I need to go more than ever.

"A promise is a promise."

## Chapter Nineteen
# Preparation

My previous jungle forays and war journalism experiences instilled in me the importance of planning, preparation and rehearsing.

Rehearsing didn't just mean testing your gear, but visualizing every scenario you might encounter and having a pre-planned solution you could pull off the shelf and implement reflexively.

In terms of gear, the most important thing was my boots and my hammock.

In terms of training, it was jungle stamina.

I believed that the training would be fairly straight forward. I dressed myself up in sweat clothes to simulate the heat and humidity of the jungle, put a pack on my back loaded with sandbags and walked up and down the thirty odd floors of my apartment building. Every week I increased the load in my back pack. I assumed that this routine would simulate the conditions I'd face in the jungle.

Additionally, I ran several miles a day with a backpack on the indoor track at my gym. Only three weeks before my departure I sprained my back and broke off the big toe nail on my right foot.

A chiropractor helped me through the worst of the back pain, and I bought a tight-fitting cloth back brace secured by Velcro. Additionally, twice a day, I soaked my back in a hot bath tub. Meanwhile, I washed out my wounded toe everyday hoping it would not get infected. The mission dates were now set and I couldn't back out because of a sore back or sore toe. Like everything else in life, when the going gets tough, the tough get going. You need to guts your way through setbacks. When you commit, you commit, no excuses.

However, walking up and down the steps of your apartment building a few hours a day is much easier than walking eight hours in the jungle, where the humidity doesn't allow the sweat to evaporate off your body and cool you down, and you're slipping and sliding up or down steep slopes with prickly bushes grabbing your body and gashing your skin.

*Spetsnaz,* the Russian Special Forces, perhaps the toughest of the tough, had an attitude about it. Pain is good. If you feel pain, it means you're still alive.

In a mail-order catalogue for camping and military gear, I surveyed the selection of boots and was sold by the U.S. Navy Seals brand name on one particular model. They were advertised as designed to do the toughest job in the most adverse conditions. Sea, air, land, street or jungle. That's what I wanted, but I should have learned my lesson from the Virgin Islands and my Navy survival knife which boasted similar advertising. But I bought them anyway.

The soles weren't grooved deep enough for a good grip, especially in jungle mud. They weren't high enough to offer good ankle support and the laces kept slipping loose even when double knotted, due to the thick padding around the ankles and tongue. Half the time, I was climbing up and down hills with my shoe laces undone.

Unfortunately, the only jungle hammock I could find in the catalogues was the same one I had used in Haiti. However, I bought one anyway. I figured it was just a question of me getting used to it. I also bought a hammock stand from a local outdoor furniture store and set it up inside my apartment so I could get used to sleeping in the hammock.

In previous years, when I was playing war correspondent, I made a point of sleeping on the hard floor in my apartment to condition my body to battle conditions. It got to the point where I preferred to sleep on the floor than in a bed. I'd check into a five-star hotel and sleep on the floor. I'd mess up the bed so it wouldn't look suspicious to the maids and management. However, I could never get used to sleeping in a hammock.

The difference between sleeping on the floor of a hard bunker and the jungle is that the jungle floor is wet, full of bugs, snakes and other things that bite you in your sleep. So, you needed to be off the ground. Even the Amazon natives did not sleep on the ground. When local Amerindians ventured too far into the rainforest and got stuck away from their villages overnight, they made hammock-like harnesses from strips of tree bark. They got rained on. But being off the ground was essential.

I always laugh when I later saw the TV shows showing survival experts making a bed out of leaves on the ground. They never show how wet and full of bug bites the guy is the next morning.

I assumed they probably helicoptered him back to a nice hotel once the cameras stopped rolling.

*Chapter Twenty*
# French Guiana Part I

French Guiana was famous for several things.

Devil's Island, where for many years France sent criminals and political prisoners. It was most notably featured in the movie *Papillon,* starring Steve McQueen and Dustin Hoffman.

Malaria and other exotic diseases.

*La Légion Étrangère.* The French Foreign Legion. They were a big presence in French Guiana. They did their jungle warfare training there and protected the base in Kourou that launched the European Space Agency's Ariane rockets and satellites. Apparently there is an advantage to launching space rockets from a position near the equator and French Guiana provided that.

The Legion also tracked down smugglers and human traffickers. Additionally, they were the front guard against neighboring countries who tried to move in on their natural resources. Gold being one of them.

French Guiana and the "X" Ted Kaufman marked on a map was an easily testable hypothesis.

So I thought.

I naively assumed that I could drop into the jungle by helicopter, walk the few miles or so to the spot, have a look around and be back in time for lunch.

I was very wrong.

Ultimately I flew to French Guiana from Chicago with an overnight stay in the Miami International Hotel. The flight from Miami made a transit stop in Port-au-Prince, Haiti, which brought back old memories.

I never met my team until I arrived in country, and took it one step at a time.

Stephane greeted me at the Cayenne airport.

He was just what you wanted in a jungle guide. He was experienced, confident, optimistic and easy going.

He confirmed that he had walked the length of French Guiana by himself and nourished himself by hunting and fishing along the way. He was originally from France but a relative got him a job in a French Guiana timber camp and he answered the call to adventure. He had a sense of humor and turned out to be a great campfire cook. He also later proved to be a good diplomat.

He also told me that we should be prepared to spend several nights in the jungle. The government only gave us permission for four days in the "closed area" and that we should make the most of it.

I had made a reservation at the Novotel, which was just outside the center of town, and booked a rental car, not knowing what to expect from taxis or public transportation.

Stephane accompanied me to my hotel where we had a beer in the lobby to discuss the expedition.

*Chapter Twenty One*

# Shopping

The next day, Stephane came by my hotel room to look over my gear. He shook his head at everything, especially my hammock. The military catalogue hammock I had brought down with me was totally inappropriate. It looked good on paper but would be a nightmare in the field.

Stephane explained that the canvas bed caused you to slip around inside and made you sweat. Second, the nice netting with tent-like roof was totally useless. When it rains in the jungle, it pours. In every direction. So the cute little tent roof on top of the netting was not going to stop anything from rushing through. I had learned this in Haiti so should have known better but didn't know what the alternative was. Also, the canvas bedding made it relatively heavy to carry.

Stephane's preferred jungle hammock was a far more simple affair and you didn't get it out of a military mail order catalogue. You bought if from a tailor shop. It was essentially a bed sheet strong enough to hold your weight with mosquito netting sewn over it. Because, it was a cotton sheet, you didn't sweat in it and you were protected from rain by sheets of plastic tarps that you set up over and around you to keep the elements out. It was also extremely light weight.

The tailor shop that custom-made my hammock also offered a nylon version, claiming it would be more waterproof, however Stephane advised that I'd not only be slipping around in it but sweating all night. So I went with the cotton bed sheet. I still hadn't learned the correct way to sleep in a hammock.

An old U.S. Special Forces friend tried to help me out and even drew a picture of the position.

"You don't do it head to foot with your back bent in the middle, but you sleep across it," he explained.

"You put your feet on one side of the hammock and your head on the other side. The hammock gets stretched out sideways across the middle and you lie on a flat sleeping surface surrounded by a cocoon that also keeps out the wind and the rain."

The military style hammock did not allow you to do that because the canvas was too stiff and narrow. It looked great in the catalogue with its tent-like tarp, but obviously the guy who designed it never spent a night in it.

I watched the tailor fabricate my hammock with bright orange colored cloth and I was surprised that the bed sheet was strong enough to hold my weight. It rolled up into a tight small sack that was also very light.

Then we went to what I'd call a Chinese "one-dollar shop." It was a small mom and pop store that carried basic home essentials like pots and pans, light bulbs, electric fans, batteries, insect repellant, toilet plungers, hardware supplies and on and on. It was only slightly bigger than a 7/11 but stocked everything. This one even sold shirts, pants and shoes.

The "one-dollar shop" designation was something I picked up in my Hong Kong days. It didn't mean you could buy anything for one dollar, but just meant that you could buy everything pretty cheaply. When I was studying Chinese I learned that over-exaggerations were often used in the language. One of my favorites was the use of the word "ten-thousand" which merely signified "many." One of my favorite restaurants in New York City's Chinatown was called "Ten Thousand Fragrances." American English also tends to exaggerate a point for dramatic effect such as "gazillions of dollars."

The Chinese had been in French Guiana for tens of years. Like most everywhere else in the world, they were imported to do all the hard, back-breaking labor that the colonials didn't want to do, but for the Chinese it was a chance at a new life away from worse hardships back home.

In French Guiana, Chinese labor was imported primarily to mine gold. Like most valuable natural resources found in underdeveloped countries around the world, gold was a double-edged sword. On the one hand, it provided jobs and foreign exchange. On the other hand, jungles were ripped down searching for it and toxic substances were used extracting it, poisoning the forests and rivers.

In the "one-dollar shop" we bought plastic bowls, eating utensils, a cooking pot, lightweight packing line to hang up our rain tarps and rubber sandals for me which Stephane advised would be necessary at the end of the day so I could take off my boots and let my feet dry out to prevent jungle rot and infection.

We then went to a grocery store and stocked up on food, mostly canned sardines and mackerel in either tomato or mustard sauce, pasta, rice, Laughing Cow cheese wedges and canned meat. I didn't notice the label on the meat, but it seemed to be the local version of Spam. Spam was an acronym meaning "shoulders of pork and ham." It was high in fat and salt, but popular during World War II and I found it quite tasty. We also bought long, loaves of French baguettes and boxes of crackers. I asked about yoghurt for breakfast, but Stephane advised that the containers would explode in the heat.

I took particular note of the "Laughing Cow" cheese wedge packaging with a smiling cow on the cover. It read *La Vache qui rit*. "The cow that laughs." Every morning when I had my Laughing Cow cheese wedges for breakfast I wondered whether the cow was laughing at me and my folly.

I also stocked up on my preferred breakfast drink, Coca-Cola. In the U.S. I grew up with Coca-Cola. My mother claimed that it was healthier than coffee because it didn't have as much caffeine, sugar and acid. She also claimed it settled your stomach. After I finished the soft drink, I could fill the plastic bottles with stream water and a water-purification tablet and they fit into my pants pockets which gave me easy access to them when I needed a sip. They made great canteens.

The next item on the list was a *topofil*.

The *topofil* was a fine thread that we would string along our path through the jungle that would allow us to back track our way out, just like Hansel and Gretel marking their path into the forest with cookie crumbs.

We went to an open market and ran into a Legionnaire in uniform. He appeared exceptionally fit and could probably haul twice his weight through the jungle. His face was rugged, tan and lined. He was likely only around thirty years old but looked like fifty. The jungle takes its toll.

Stephane asked him where we could buy a *topofil* and he directed us toward another part of the market. Apparently the Legion also relied on this low-tech navigation system in the jungle.

Separately, Stephane was keen on finding a particular brand of local rum. I didn't know why but we checked several stores yet he rejected most of them. Maybe it was the taste or maybe the alcohol content.

"What's the rum for? Snake bites?" I asked Stephane somewhat jokingly, now a bit worried.

"Conviviality," he responded with a smile.

Now, I was even more worried, but didn't think one bottle could cause too many problems or too much conviviality.

As we were driving back through town toward my hotel, I noted a bar and restaurant along the road called La Bodega. It appeared to have outdoor seating and looked like quite a nice place to grab a bite or drink.

"That's where all the Legionnaires hang out," Stephane indicated.

I wanted to take a look, but Stephane suggested we wait until we get back from the jungle.

I dropped Stephane off at a house that he was sharing with friends, then went back to my hotel and started to take inventory of my gear and again re-rehearse plans both on the maps and in my head.

As I was driving back, I got an unexpected morale boost from the car radio. It was playing a *zouk*-like song in French Creole. I couldn't understand any of the lyrics except the reprise at the end which was, *Ce n'est pas difficile*. "It is not difficult." It became my mission to find this song as soon as I got back from the jungle.

The first thing I did when I got back to the hotel was draw a hot bath and soak my back in it. It was tight and painful. After three weeks in a chiropractor's office, it was still not right. It always seems when you really want something, obstacles are thrown up in your path to make you prove that you really want it. After soaking my back for half an hour, I cleaned out my wounded big toe. I then ordered a light dinner from room service and took a melatonin table to get me to sleep. I had trouble falling asleep since I was a small child and melatonin allegedly distilled the sleep-inducing ingredient in chicken soup and warm milk called tryptophan. It was sold over the counter as a vitamin supplement.

It worked, but only for three hours. Then you were wide awake for the rest of the night, even if you took another tablet. I swallowed one after dinner along with an ibuprofen for my back pain and tried to sleep.

I did deep-breathing exercises and focused on positive images of me finding the plane in the jungle. I also focused on images of Grammy and tried to feel her there with me.

*Chapter Twenty Two*
# Insertion

The next morning I picked up Stephane in my rental car and drove to the airport where I met Pierre for the first time as well as the helicopter pilot Martel.

Martel was just what you'd expect from a jungle pilot. He wore a light blue zipped down jump suit and had a cheerful, daring and optimistic attitude against all odds. French Guiana's Han Solo.

Pierre was more no-nonsense. He methodically checked all the equipment and carefully interrogated Stephane about the plan. He was prepared to fly on a mission sight unseen but not totally blind. He wore a thick cotton long-sleeved shirt with a German flag on it, long jungle pants and lightweight sneaker-like jungle boots. Because of the flag, I asked if he had served in the German army, but he just replied that it was a good shirt.

Meanwhile, Stephane wore a similar outfit but I noted that he had long, shin length rubber boots the Brits would call "Wellingtons."

"These are the best," he explained. "But you need to get used to them. Your feet will not fit in them very well but they will keep out the water and mud."

All their gear was packed in large, white plastic jars with tight red screw-on lids called *tukes*. The *tuke* was about twelve inches wide and twenty-five inches high. It protected everything inside from rain and humidity.

The jars were bought from local Chinese restaurants, which used them to store meat. I could not find the word *tuke* in a French dictionary so have no idea where it came from or what it really meant.

The *tukes* were then slipped into large duffel bags with only shoulder straps. The straps had no padding and the bags no back support. I couldn't image these guys hiking through the jungle with heavy plastic jars bouncing against their back. But they did it. I picked one up and estimated it weighed about sixty pounds, whereas my padded, waist-belted, custom-fitted frame pack weighed only about forty-five pounds. But it was grueling to carry up and down slippery slopes in the heat and humidity.

In the meantime, a local journalist showed up from the national newspaper. I thought it would be good publicity and cooperated as much as I could. In the end, he put me on the front page of the national newspaper, which probably said more about the daily news in French Guiana than the importance of my story. But I was very appreciative. If Larry wanted to come out of hiding, this was his chance.

After everything was checked and loaded, we took some pictures then got onboard.

I sat up front next to the pilot while Stephane and Pierre sat in the back. The ride reminded me of other helicopter experiences. The thing vibrated like crazy and there was no sense of forward motion. At any moment, you felt you would drop out of the sky like a stone.

Before landing, we overflew the destination site but could see nothing. The jungle canopy was high and impenetrable. It was like looking down into broccoli.

We then flew past *Pic du Croissant*. *Pic du Croissant* had the long clearing I spotted from the mapping agency photographs and thought it might be a makeshift runway. But it was clearly just a large erosion on the side of the mountain. I also didn't see anything that looked like an airplane fuselage.

The pilot ultimately landed on a very small rocky outcrop protruding from the jungle, however it was not an ideal landing zone. The pilot needed to wiggle the chopper in, cutting off the branches of some small trees with its rotor blades in the process. When we finally touched ground, the pilot pulled out a map and poured over it with Stephane and Pierre.

While they were preoccupied with the map, I walked over into a clear space and tried to get a GPS fix. Luckily I got one. Unfortunately, it indicated that we were about five to six miles from our destination. Twelve miles round trip.

My plan for getting to X was to go due west until we reached Crique Alina, which was not just a creek but more like a small river. It would be a good landmark and we could follow it north to X. Also, we'd be on high ground most of the way and not have to crawl up and down densely vegetated jungle hills.

However, Pierre disagreed.

He claimed it was difficult to follow rivers here because there were no river banks. The jungle reached right down to the water's edge and the vegetation was thick. So it was not like a stroll along the beach. Also, the rivers were infested with Caimans, small alligators that could pop up out of nowhere, grab your leg and drag you into the water for dinner.

"We need to go straight for the spot," he asserted.

A straight shot would only be about four miles. Eight miles round trip and save us four miles of hacking our way through the bush.

So I took the advice of the experts, but later learned that you always need to take expert advice with a grain of salt.

Expertise is great but judgment is everything.

*Chapter Twenty Three*

# Trek

The helicopter took off and left us in the middle of nowhere.

For safety reasons, Stephane brought only one machete that he would carry. The humidity made the handle slippery and it could easily fly out of your hand and slash the teammate in front of you or behind.

Ironically, his machete was the same thin-bladed, plastic handled flimsy sort that I had bought in U.S. camping equipment stores and took to the Virgin Islands and Haiti.

After the chopper took off, Stephane knelt down and slid the machete's edges back and forth on the rocks to sharpen it. Then we headed off into the dense jungle. Stephane was in the lead, followed by me with my compass and maps, then Pierre with the *topofil*, the reel of thin, lightweight thread that he'd string along behind us so we could find our way back.

I didn't bother with my back brace because I thought it would be too hot. I just tightened the waist strap on my backpack and sucked up the lower back pain. It was only pain. At least I could walk.

Just before we entered the bush, Pierre spotted some animal poo.

"Jaguar," he noted.

"How can you tell?" I asked.

"Because it has broken bones in it from the animals it ate," he replied. "If it is vegetarian, there would be no animal bones in it."

"Are we in danger from them?" I followed up.

"No," he returned. "Since this is a closed area, they have probably never seen humans. They are probably tracking us from a distance out of curiosity, but would not attack because we are bigger than them."

Later, I learned that jaguars do in fact attack animals bigger than them.

"Our biggest danger is from wild boar, bees and trees," he explained. "The wild boar run in packs and trample anything in their way. So when you set up your hammock tonight you need to make sure it is at least three feet off the ground. The bees also attack in packs. They are from Africa, deadly and very smart. If you jump into a river to escape them, they will wait for you to come out from the water, then attack you. I hope you are not allergic to them."

"And what about the trees?" I asked. "I've never been attacked by a tree before and think I can outrun one," I added with a smirk.

"This is the rainforest," Pierre continued. "Everything is living and dying at the same time. The dying, rotten trees will fall down without warning and crush you. If you hear a crashing sound, you need to get out of the way.

"You will see. Everything is attacking everything else, trying to survive, even the plants."

"The plants?" I asked almost jokingly. "I never thought that I might be killed by a flower."

"You will see," Pierre went on. "They will be scratching you for your blood, which is food for them. Also, if their vines trip you up and you fall on your head and die, it is good fertilizer for them."

So, it began.

As soon as we entered the rainforest, I realized how easy it was to get lost. You were surrounded by super-tall trees and thick vegetation. Visibility was maybe six feet. Although Stephane was only maybe ten feet ahead of me, I easily lost sight of him. Pierre, who was in the rear, seemed to instinctively know where we were and took time to tie his reel of *topofil* thread onto bushes and trees high enough so we could easily see it on the way back and it wouldn't be lost in the undergrowth.

Stephane noted that the secret to surviving in the jungle was to avoid contact with it. You want to walk around obstacles, not through them and avoid using your machete as much as possible because using it will only tire you out. If you get tired, you will sit down, fall asleep and die. The snakes, spiders, ants and plants will feast on you. Then the other animals.

As noted, given the limited time of only four days granted by the government, Pierre suggested we make a straight line for X regardless of what was in our path. As it turned out, what was in our path was extremely dense jungle, prickly bushes, razor grass, and grueling hills with muddy, slippery slopes. Stephane and Pierre had no problem with it, but it was very tough on me who only climbed apartment steps in preparation. But we stayed true to the compass course. It was typically impossible to get a GPS fix given the high treetops blocking out the sky.

As a back up, we counted the small creeks that we crossed along the way. The topographic maps I got from the Paris agency showed the tiniest of streams and they still seemed to be true to the terrain although the maps were made in the 1950s.

Also, due to the high canopy, the jungle was dark. Every picture I took required the flash. On the positive side, the high canopy protected us from the direct sunlight that would have exacerbated the draining heat and humidity.

Although this was the end of the rainy season, it still rained a fair bit. It started and stopped without warning. I had packed rain gear, but the first time I put it on, the nylon fabric made me sweat like a sauna. I was soaking wet all the time, so the rain gear didn't matter and was more of an inconvenience. I never used it again. However, the raindrops bouncing off the top of my head was like Chinese water torture. Fortunately, I quickly found I could deal with the dripping on my head just by putting on a cap.

When we stopped for a break, I pulled out my water pump to filter stream water into my bottles. However, this gadget was such a nuisance to set up, keep the parts together and make them work, that I buried it in the jungle somewhere and resorted to the water purification tablets I had brought along as backup. They turned the water brown and gave it a nasty chemical taste, but I got used to it. When you're dying of thirst, you can get used to anything.

Stephane noted that these pumps are useful only when you are staying at a campsite for a long time and not on the move every day.

For their part, Stephane and Pierre just drank water directly from the streams. They'd fold up leaves from some bush into cups and scoop the water out. They claimed that the acid content in the streams was high enough to kill any germs. But I was not convinced. I never drank tap water anywhere in the world, even in the U.S., and avoided salads because you never knew what bacteria they harbored or the quality of the water the staff washed them with.

Years ago a colleague was in the hospital and it was touch-and-go for weeks because she had contracted typhus from a salad bar in a five-star hotel in Southeast Asia.

The water purification tablets required 20 minutes to be effective, so I had two water bottles and timed them accordingly with my Timex Ironman watch. Great for the big numbers and bright Indigo light it shone on the dial.

Stephane made a point of limiting our rest stops to five minutes so we didn't get too comfortable and lose the will to march forward or doze off. At each stop, he magically produced a fresh orange from his pack that I savored slowly over the full five minutes.

Despite six months of climbing up and down stairs in my Chicago apartment building in a sweat suit with a backpack full of sand bags, I was not in shape for the rigors of the rainforest. Many times my heart was beating so strongly, I thought it would burst out of my chest. But Stephane and Pierre tolerated me and when I begged to stop for a minute, they let me stop. Sometimes they gave me two minutes to allow my heartbeat to slow down but never longer.

At least my Vietnam jungle boots performed. They didn't keep out the water, but they gave me the support I needed to go up and down the hills.

Years earlier, I had read in a book about British SAS tactics that you shouldn't bathe in the jungle. The SAS or Special Air Services were the elite of the elite special forces in any country and "knew best" on matters of survival in all terrains. The book even suggested that you pee in your pants because exposing yourself to the jungle would put you at risk of vermin that might swim up the urine stream into your penis. Particularly, you should also avoid peeing in the water because parasites would be attracted to the warm urine, enter your penis and lay eggs.

The book even criticized an American Special Forces officer assigned to their jungle training team for washing himself every day.

"You need to build up an oily, dirty crust on your skin," one British training instructor told him. "Not only will it keep the insects off, but it will keep you warm at night."

The American officer ignored their advice, later came down with a high fever of unknown causes and had to be evacuated out by helicopter.

Between the humidity and the sweat of my exertion, I was soaking wet all the time. So peeing in my pants would not make a difference and if the SAS could do it, I could do it. I tried it, but it didn't feel right. Not only did I wet my already wet pants, but the urine dripped down into my socks and boots. But I gave it a fair shot.

I also read that U.S. troops in Vietnam didn't wear any underwear to reduce excess sweat in their crotch area and the subsequent rashes it would induce.

So for two days I didn't bathe, peed in my pants without underwear and felt miserable while my nylon tropical hiking trousers scraped against my groin causing considerable irritation. Meanwhile, my partners washed themselves and their clothes in a nearby stream every day. The humidity was so intense that you'd never have any dry clothes to put on in the morning. If you washed your clothes, they wouldn't dry out overnight and were still wet and cold the next morning but at least they were clean and after an hour trekking in the jungle, everything was hot and wet anyway.

I later asked an American ex-Special Forces friend who had operated behind enemy lines during the Vietnam War for his thoughts. Essentially, he endorsed the French point of view.

"If you're sneaking around the jungle through enemy lines, you don't bathe because it would expose you to the enemy. Also, the smell of the soap would make it easier for them to track you. They could also track you based on your body smell and the imprint of your boots. So, I never wore American boots. But if you're not being tracked by the bad guys, you might want to take a bath."

Also, he indicated that the only time he peed in his pants was during his first mortar attack.

Growing up as an East Coast American, I was indoctrinated into British heritage, and tended to trust them on everything as father knows best. But, at least in this situation, the French knew better. We were not being attacked, tracked or shot at and I ultimately followed their example of washing myself and my clothes every day thereafter. I felt much better.

The next day, I put on underpants and the next time I needed to pee, I just unzipped my fly and peed on the ground like a normal guy. Also, apparently the U.S. troops in Vietnam wore soft cotton trousers and not scratchy nylon ones.

Meanwhile, Pierre constantly criticized me for touching the trees and bushes, indicating I could get an infection even though I was wearing gloves. However, I couldn't make it up and down the slippery slopes without grabbing onto something for assistance. My knees were under a huge strain and I was the oldest member of the team. Forty-five years old. I thought I had protected my hands with the thick leather work gloves I was wearing, but when I took them off, I found that my hands were covered with hundreds of minute splinters and the gloves were already rotting due to the jungle humidity.

We hiked the entire day, just following the compass needle but not really knowing where we were going. When I was in sailing school, I was always taught to trust your compass. So we assumed that we were hiking northwest and getting closer to X. As dusk approached, Stephane recommended that we set up camp for the night.

Stephane was very particular about where he set up camp. It needed to be on flat ground and close to a stream where everyone could wash up and there was good cooking water. He liked a spot we stumbled into as the sun was setting, so we dropped our stuff and set up for the night. We felt we were close to our mark so this could be used as a base camp where we left most of our heavy gear, including the canned food and the next day we could sprint with light loads to X.

After setting up my hammock, I took off my boots and socks, and slipped into my sandals to let my feet dry out. Additionally, Pierre advised I string up my boots on my hammock lines, shake them vigorously the next morning and meticulously check them for spiders and snakes before I stick my feet back into them. I never found any snakes, but sometimes one or two spiders.

I couldn't believe how much energy Stephane and Pierre had after the day's ordeal. They methodically went about chopping wood for the campfire, preparing food, and setting up protective rain tarps over our hammocks. Just tying up my hammock was an effort and Stephane reminded me to make sure it was at least three feet off the ground in case our camp was over-run by wild pigs during the night.

Stephane made a nice meal over the campfire and we toasted with an apéritif he called *Petite Punch*. It consisted of a spot of the local rum he so carefully sought out, brown sugar, a wedge of lime and canteen water. We drank it from the plastic bowls we got at the Chinese "one-dollar-shop."

He was very sparing with the rum, and poured us less than a shot. However, it was enough to take the edge off the day's trek as well as the chill off the cold night jungle air.

While we were eating dinner a large sci-fi, tarantula-type spider strolled into our camp. In fact, it walked right in front of me. No one seemed concerned. Stephane just swatted it away with the back of his hand.

I then went back to my hammock, wrote some notes, planned the route for the next day and settled in for the night. My sweat suit was not sufficient to keep out the damp and cold. I should have known better from my previous jungle experience but hadn't prepared for the cold night. I had no other dry clothes in my pack so just curled up into a ball and tried to stay warm. But between the damp cold and the noise of the jungle, I got little sleep.

Jungles are noisy places at night. Insects fill the air with screeching sounds. Then the birds chime in. I assumed that the birds were after the insects so they should stay quiet while they hunted the bugs, but they didn't. One I dubbed the Beethoven bird because his call was like the opening of Beethoven's fifth symphony. *"Bum, Bum, Bum, Baam."*

He went at it all night.

Trees crashed in the night but none seemed close and I couldn't be bothered to leave the hammock. I popped a melatonin pill for sleep, which only knocked me out for a couple of hours and a Lariam tablet, an anti-malarial prophylactic.

Lariam was prescribed by my doctor as the anti-malarial agent I needed for French Guiana. Apparently, depending on where you are traveling, a different malarial medication is prescribed based on who the mosquitoes are. However, Lariam came with significant side-effect warnings. Specifically, hallucinations, nightmares and blurred or loss of vision.

I had no nightmares, but my short-range vision was severely compromised. I needed to look at my maps using the tiny magnifying glass attached to my Swiss Army knife. It took me four or five weeks to regain my normal vision once I stopped taking the drug. Fortunately, there are now newer drugs for malaria prevention. I got no sleep for the rest of the night and struggled with the cold, damp air while trying to get comfortable in the hammock.

*Chapter Twenty Four*
# Jungle Navigation

I never trusted navigating by technology.

When I was a sailing student, I learned how to take compass bearings, make corrections based on magnetic deviation and account for the tides. This served me well on various sailing adventures throughout the Caribbean and the Mediterranean.

I later took a course in celestial navigation, which teaches you how to find your spot on the globe using a sextant to measure sun, star and planet angles.

In practice, celestial navigation required meticulous measurements that were very difficult to get right standing on dry land, let alone on top of a bouncing boat in the high seas. However, it was a very enriching course that opened up my eyes to our place in the universe and how time could be equated to distance.

At minimum, I could tell from the sky, day or night, which way I was going even without all the complex math. Of course, in the middle of the rain forest you couldn't see the sky.

The new, hot technology at the time was GPS or the global positioning system. Based on a small hand-held receiver interacting with satellites in the sky you could get a quick latitude and longitude of your position. The receiver calculated your distance from the satellites based on built-in real-time maps of their locations and the time it took their signal to reach your device. A friend and his wife sailed around the world only using a small GPS receiver and no knowledge of celestial navigation.

I asked them what they'd do if the GPS got wet and failed or the batteries ran out.

"We have a backup receiver sealed in a waterproof plastic container with fresh batteries," came the confident reply. They sailed around the world three times on last count, so I guess that was fine.

It might be okay sailing across the sea navigating by GPS. However, there was a problem hiking through a forest or jungle. GPS required a clear, open sky and at least three satellites above you with a direct line of sight to your receiver in order to fix your position. You needed four satellites for an altitude fix.

Nevertheless, I bought the latest model handheld receiver, but was concerned about whether it would work in a jungle where you typically have over one hundred foot canopies and no skylight. Also, South America was not a priority for the satellite companies so they typically didn't have a lot of them up there covering those skies.

I called up the manufacturer and asked to speak to someone in technical support and explained the situation.

"No problem," a cheerful, energetic female with a perfect phone voice exuded from the other side. Obviously, she was just a salesperson whose job was to make customers happy with their purchase whether it worked or not.

In the world of terrestrial navigation there is "true north" and "magnetic north."

True north was the direction posted on a paper map and directly pointed to the North Pole. However, because the earth's magnetic field is not consistent around the globe, what you read on your magnetic compass might or might not be close to true north depending on where you were in the world. To make it more complicated, the deviation could swing your compass either east or west of true north and magnetic north migrated around the pole a bit every year.

When I was a student of marine navigation, we were taught the rhyme "East is least, West is best." I think it meant that east was a negative deviation and west meant a positive one. Or did it mean that you subtract degrees when the deviation is East and add them when it was West? You tend to forget these things when you really need them.

I never thought about it when navigating on a boat, because the compass rose on the charts showed the magnetic headings overlaid on top of the true ones, so you could just align your chart rulers and plotters accordingly and not worry about whether you were supposed to add or subtract the reading on your compass to get the true heading. So, you just sailed the magnetic course on your compass.

Larry's chart gave both the true and magnetic readings for their courses at the time, so navigation should not have been a problem for them. The deviation was about eleven degrees at the time, which was pretty significant.

As noted, when I was in French Guiana, the magnetic deviation was even more significant. Around fifteen to seventeen degrees West. And since I was using topographic charts which did not have the dual compass rose like nautical charts, doing the math correctly was critical. If you added instead of subtracted or vice-versa, you could be thirty degrees off course.

In the jungle, I also learned that it was virtually impossible to get a GPS fix because of the high, dense treetops. In addition, if you managed to lock onto three satellites, the fix might last for only a second, as one satellite moved out of sight. So, you needed to be quick about it.

Later, I learned that the compass was also not reliable even when accounting for magnetic deviation. Apparently, French Guiana has a lot of various ore in the ground, so our compass course was additionally deviated in a way we could not have predicted or measured. The published charts showed the offshore deviation which is all that ships and planes cared about.

But the charts also indicated incalculable "magnetic anomalies" onshore. So I could easily see Uncle Larry's plane getting deviated off course once it made landfall. So if our compass bearings were off in the jungle due to various ores in the ground, we would have no way of knowing it.

The morning after our night in the base camp, we climbed up a nearby hill to try to find out where we were using the GPS. I briefly got a satellite fix and found out that we weren't where we thought we were.

Based on the compass, we had marched directly northwest toward our objective and were very close to our destination. But the GPS fix indicated we were still miles away and in the wrong direction. We had been hiking directly west towards Crique Alina.

In one way, this was good, because we could continue onwards to the creek and follow it north as I had thought best. On the other hand, it meant we were still very far from our destination.

"Okay. Here's the plan," I said with some sense of command. "The straight line route isn't working. The GPS is limited in use and the compass is unreliable. So we're going to go west to Crique Alina which will give us a landmark. Then, we'll follow the creek north from there."

Pierre and Stephane consented.

The way to Crique Alina was actually very pleasant. We were on high ground and there wasn't much jungle to storm through. But once we descended to the creek, Pierre was right. There was no river bank and it was flanked by thick reeds, razor grass and other jungle growth. We had to go inland to make any progress, which involved much hacking with the machete. It was very slow going.

In the meantime, we ran out of string, so we had no bread crumbs left to find our way back home.

Stephane suggested that the jungle might be less dense on the other side, so he and Pierre crossed over, balancing themselves along a large fallen log, while I remained behind and awaited the verdict.

After crossing the creek, Stephane shouted,"I think we found something." And he started banging his machete on something metallic.

I shinnied across the creek along the log, not wanting to lose my balance and fall into the creek with all of my gear.

Meanwhile, Stephane was scraping the dirt away from what appeared to be a large sheet of metal. However, it was not a sheet of aircraft aluminum. It was a heavy piece of iron with a railroad wheel attached. It appeared to be some sort of mining cart. So, we left it and continued north. In fact, after we got through a dense patch of high razor grass, it became easier going and felt like we'd soon been upon X.

However, at around three o'clock in the afternoon, both Stephane and Pierre were very concerned that we should start heading back in order to reach base camp before dark. We had been hiking since dawn, so it could take us another nine hours to get back to the camp.

There were several concerns. First, that we would not be able to pick up the remains of the *topofil* trail, and be stumbling around in the dark.

Second, the wild life.

"We need to cross Crique Alina before night or the Caimans will be waiting for us," Stephan cautioned. "It will be very risky. The Caimans are very dangerous."

Unfortunately, the idea of a Base Camp was maybe a bad idea. If we had carried all our gear and food with us, we could camp out where we were and perhaps make it to X the next morning. But now it was too late for that. I trusted the compass and the compass was wrong. We had nothing to eat and nowhere to sleep. I suggested that I was fine with the crackers and water in my back pack and could sleep on the ground for one night. However, Stephane and Pierre both stressed that it was not a good idea to sleep on the ground. Never mind about jaguars and snakes, all the insects will feed on you. We needed to get back to base camp.

I urged the guys to give me five minutes. I would leave all my gear with them except for a water bottle and camera. I told them I would jog a compass course for exactly five minutes, then turnaround and jog back along the reverse course. We were too close to stop now.

However, after jogging for only about two minutes, I was confronted with a huge, impenetrable wall of jungle. It appeared as if someone, out of spite, had intentionally erected a barricade of dense, intertwined vegetation to keep me from going any further. The jungle was laughing at me. The Laughing Cow cheese was laughing at me. I wanted to drop down to my knees and cry.

I walked back to the team and they were anxious to get going.

We found our way back to a crossing point at Crique Alina, based on all the slashing we had done through the forest. Fortunately, it was not yet dark. However, Stephane noted Caiman tracks along the river bank.

"We need to cross quickly," he urged.

We couldn't find the log we had previously used to get across the creek, so we just waded in chest-high water through the river. Fortunately, without incident.

But the rest of the trek back was exceptionally grueling. After we crossed Crique Alina, we needed to crawl up the muddy hills we had slid down earlier in the day.

At night.

We all strapped on head lamps but could only really see a few footsteps in front of us.

One hill was particularly challenging for me. Every time I made four steps forward, I slipped back five. I was mentally and physically exhausted and ready to lie down and die. I felt the worst thing was to die alone in the jungle. But I just didn't have the energy to continue. It was cold, muddy and wet, but I didn't care. I couldn't take it any more and just wanted to die and get it all over with. I didn't even shout out to my team mates.

I made myself comfortable in the cold, wet mud and was ready to give up and go to sleep forever. Then I felt an enormous, warm, glowing feeling surrounding me and the presence of Grammy.

"I already lost one son in the jungle and I'm not going to lose another," she scolded me angrily. "So, git up and git a move on." She always spelled and pronounced "get" as "git" which made it a stronger point.

"Git going," she shouted at me forcefully.

"Git!"

"Git!"

I crouched for a minute in the shin deep mud, then found the strength to slowly make my way up the hill inch by inch. I occasionally slipped back down the muddy slope, but pushed forward.

I don't know if I was driven by determination, fear or love.

Stephane and Pierre were already at the top of the hill waiting for me. They were unaware of my struggle and I didn't share it with them.

"We found the *topofil,*" Stephane said joyfully.

When you shined your head lamp on it, it appeared as a guiding ray of light in the otherwise dark, dense, forbidding jungle.

There was now hope, and this simple low-tech tool brought us back home to our base camp.

Everyone immediately dropped their packs and sat down on the nearest log. Stephane pulled out a pack of Gauloises Reds, the full-flavored variety, lit one up, inhaled deeply, then mixed everyone our evening ration of *Petite Punch*.

I savored mine slowly and felt a warmth wind its way through my body and dissolve the cold, damp jungle night air.

Pierre quickly finished his then switched to tea. I watched his hands tremble as he brought the cup to his mouth.

"Don't worry," he said. "We'll go back tomorrow and find your airplane."

That gave us only a day to get there and back to the helicopter rendezvous. We'd have to cover twice the distance we covered over two days in just one day.

I knew they could do it, but I could not. And if I faltered, they would die trying to get me back.

Pierre caught me watching his shaking hands.

"It could be a lot worse, you know," he stated.

"How so," I asked, not being able to imagine anything worse than this.

"Someone could be shooting at us," he replied.

I immediately took this to heart and thought about American soldiers during the Vietnam War who lived in these horrible conditions every day for months on end getting shot at and bombed with mortars and artillery, not to mention mines and booby traps along every trail they walked. It gave me new respect for the military.

I made a decision.

"You know," I announced to Stephane and Pierre, "The last thing I want to do is to come back here and do this all over again," I said. "But I'd rather have a successful reconnaissance than a fatal mission.

"Tonight, we're going to get a good night's sleep and tomorrow we're going home.

"I am the weak link in this chain. I know you guys can do it, but I can't. And I know that if I fall and break something, you guys will do everything to get me out of the jungle or die trying. And I don't want to compromise your safety."

They meekly smiled. They seemed indifferent about staying or going, but I felt it was the right decision.

After the rum kicked in, I had enough strength to get out of my wet jungle wear and slip into my dinner sweat suit.

In the process, I also noticed a large tick attached to my left leg.

According to what I read, you removed a tick by putting a cigarette to it or pouring alcohol on it. This induced the tick to release the probe it injected into your skin to suck out the blood.

Pierre said otherwise. He claimed those techniques didn't work and you needed to tightly grab the base of the probe as close to the skin as possible and pull it out. However, when I tried to do this, the probe broke off and a big piece was left underneath my skin.

"Don't worry," he explained. "It is now only like a splinter and will be forced out as your skin heals."

Later, the area around the probe became a pus-filled pimple and I was able to squeeze out the probe with the pus. For years I had a black mark there, which later became a red mark. But it's still there.

I should have tried the cigarette approach first. I noted earlier that as we walked through the jungle, Pierre had picked up some leeches on his chest. But he just cut them off with a knife leaving patches of smeared blood in their place. Again, I had read you're supposed to put a cigarette to the leech's head, which will cause it to release its grip and drop off.

Two reasons to take up smoking in the jungle.

*Chapter Twenty Five*
# Homeward Bound

The next morning we started back towards the helicopter landing zone. Three quarters of the way there, I needed to stop. I was exhausted and dozing off into sleep as I walked. It was not only the trek and backpack that wore heavily on me but the lack of sleep in the hammock.

I was overwhelmed by the need to sleep. I didn't have any physical strength left and was very sleep deprived. Between the screeching insects, the Beethoven bird and the awkwardness of sleeping in a hammock, I was getting only about two to three hours a night. At home, I typically got nine. I told them I needed to take a nap. They said I couldn't do that until we made camp.

Stephane instructed me to stay behind with Pierre while he went ahead to look for a campsite. I sat down and propped my back up against a tree while Pierre kept talking to me to keep me from dozing off. I'm sure at some point he'd start slapping me if I didn't respond.

Fortunately, after only a short wait, Stephane returned indicating he had found a place he liked. It was on flat ground and near a stream. Pierre took my backpack and wore it on his chest.

As soon as we got to the campsite, Stephane gave me a shot of rum and sugar water. He strung up my hammock and I went into a deep sleep. I woke up after a nice nap to the smell of Stephane's campfire cooking.

Then I went down to the stream, took a bath and washed myself and my clothes as they did. And I was glad about my decision to go home.

We had two rations of rum that night and everyone got a good night's sleep. Even me. Occasionally I was woken up by the sound of a crashing tree, but it was off in the distance and no threat to our camp.

The next morning, we had our typical breakfast of hot tea, crackers and Laughing Cow cheese wedges, then headed off for the LZ. We picked up bits of the *topofil* again and that encouraged everyone that we were on the right track and took the pressure off of me to navigate.

The pilot said he would fly in around noon, wait several hours, then fly out. It was too risky to keep the chopper on the ground too long. He'd try again the next day if we weren't there. I brought along several handheld camping radios and gave one to the pilot. But the radio range was not sufficient to permit contact until we were already in sight of each other.

We arrived early, but the wait was unbearable. Again, I thought back again to American GIs during the Vietnam War waiting to get airlifted out of a hot landing zone as the enemy pounded them with shells, splattered them with bullets while they wondered whether the chopper would really show up and when. Would the chopper really get there or was it diverted somewhere else more urgent?

In the meantime, I suddenly found the urge to take a dump. It's interesting how you can pee under almost any circumstances, but you can't take a dump unless you feel safe and secure. I found that many of my sailing friends could not take a dump on a boat, even if we were at sea for a week, despite a decent toilet with a closed door.

I hadn't had a bowel movement in four days, and felt I could not wait any longer. However, the challenge would be doing it in the Asian-style squat position. It was never clear to me how you could hold that painful position as well as avoid dumping everything into your rolled-down pants. Girls pee in the outdoors this way all the time, I said to myself, so it must be okay. I should have asked my girlfriends to teach me.

I walked around the rocks and found a sloped area that I thought might draw the excrement away from me. I rolled my trousers down around my boots and miraculously, everything that came out missed both trousers and boots.

As soon as I stood up, the insects were all over it in seconds. I thought it was very polite of them to wait until I was finished.

Shortly thereafter, we heard the thumping of helicopter rotors in the distance. French pilot Martel was on time, even though he didn't expect us to be there. He circled the LZ a few times and Pierre took a position in front of the rocks, directing him like an air traffic controller so he could weave his way through the trees.

Martel showed up with the same reporter from the national daily newspaper, who did a very nice piece about our effort even though we only found some scrap metal and not an airplane.

We got back to the airport, loaded up my car and I dropped everyone off amidst sad farewells.

But I had another mission.

*Chapter Twenty Six*
# La Bodega

Ever since Stephane and I drove past the La Bodega bar in Cayenne and he told me that's where the Legionnaires hung out, I was on a mission to have at least one beer there.

But I hadn't brought a change of clothes with me. I wanted to keep my pack as light as possible and make sure it would fit into my economy class overhead airline compartment so it wouldn't get lost with other baggage. I only had a short window of time and couldn't take any chances that the airline would lose my gear. However, my current clothes stank of jungle and sweat and I had nothing to change into while the hotel washed them.

I took my first hot shower in a week then put on my stinking clothes. For shoes I used my rubber sandals then drove into town and went back to the Chinese "one-dollar" shop where Stephane and I had bought plastic bowls, utensils, packing cord to string up our tarps and other supplies.

The "one-dollar" shop welcomed me with open arms and we exchanged some hellos in Cantonese. They loved the fact that I could speak a bit of their language. I needed new pants, a shirt, socks and some shoes.

They had only loud, Hawaiian-style shirts but that would have to do. The only pants that fit me were white jeans with legs too long so the shop hemmed them up with a stapler. The only thing that fit comfortably on my swollen feet were blue suede moccasins. "Loafers" in American-speak.

When I was all dressed up, I looked like I had just fallen off of a cruise liner.

But I was focused on the mission, confidant and not deterred.

I drove back to the hotel, sent my smelly jungle clothes to the hotel laundry, took another shower, then dressed up in my new outfit and drove to La Bodega.

When I showed up in the bar, I saw in my peripheral vision that a lot of heads turned, but I didn't acknowledge them. Serious looking guys with short haircuts and arms bigger than my legs filled the tables. They were all sipping some kind of spirit out of small glasses and talking quietly among themselves.

Judging by the milky color, the drink was *pastis*, a French licorice-tasting liqueur similar to *ouzo, arak* or *sambuca*. It was flavored with *anise* and typically had an alcohol content of forty to fifty percent.

I ignored the stares and confidently walked up to the bar, where I was greeted by a dark woman of mixed race with exceptionally large breasts bulging out of a tank-top T-shirt. Braless. She planted her breasts on the counter in front of me and in French asked me what I wanted.

What a tease.

I noticeably looked at her breasts and smiled.

She smiled back.

Meanwhile, I noted that everyone in the room was still observing me out of the corner of their eyes, trying to figure who I was and what I was up to.

*"Une bière,"* I said. "A beer."

*"Quel genre de bière?"* she asked. "What kind of beer?"

I didn't want to draw attention to myself by ordering something off the drinks list and appearing to be a non-local though obviously my garb read "tourist" in neon lights. I spied a poster on the wall for the Belgian beer Stella Artois and responded accordingly. I liked Stella, so there was no sacrifice on my part.

*"Une Stella,"* I noted. "A Stella."

Then she said something in French I didn't catch, except for the last phrase asking me if there was a problem ordering it.

*"Un problèm?"* She asked. "Any problem?"

*"Pas de problèm,"* I quickly replied not wanting to make a fuss, but also not knowing what she had said.

But that answer immediately turned all heads and eyes on me and the otherwise silent mouths started chattering among themselves. I didn't realize what the problem was until I tasted the beer. It was non-alcoholic.

In my travels, I found that in many cultures, mostly European, if you order a drink, it must be alcoholic, otherwise it's not a "real" drink and you are offending the friend who offered to buy it as well as all the other drinkers in the bar. I learned this the hard way when I was living in Hong Kong and my expat friends invited me out but could not accept the fact that I might order a Coke or Perrier even if I might be on antibiotics for some infection and was not supposed to drink alcohol.

"That's not a drink, mate," was often the reply. "If you're not going to drink with us, best you just go home."

Under those conditions, I typically went home.

Meanwhile, they stayed in the bars drinking until they threw up, then moved on to other bars where they drank until they threw up some more.

Many bars in Hong Kong stayed open all night long, so you could do a lot of drinking and heaving in one evening. At six in the morning, they'd go home, take a nap for a few hours, a quick shower, then off to the office. They all had techniques for making it through the work day.

Typically, it involved telling the secretary they were off to a meeting, then finding an empty stall in the men's restroom where they locked themselves in, and leaned their heads on a pile of rolled up toilet paper for a few hours to sleep it off.

The goal was to make it to lunch, which was typically accompanied by a glass of wine or pint of beer that relieved the hangover. They faked their way through the afternoon, then started the evening all over again.

A journalist friend referred to them as "minstrels."

"There are two kinds of expats in Hong Kong," he explained. "Minstrels and Exiles. Minstrels are typically here on two-year corporate contracts. They sing their song, party hard and get reassigned to the next destination. They don't care where they are as long as the pay package is good. Exiles are here for the long haul. They are fascinated by Hong Kong and Asia, learn the languages and stay on after their contracts run out, which means they end up scrounging out a living here for the rest of their lives and die in poverty."

American companies preferred non-Americans such as Brits, Australians and Canadians, while British companies hired British, Chinese companies Chinese, German companies Germans and so on. American companies hired Brits, Canadians and Aussies because they spoke English and didn't have to file all the complicated, intrusive paperwork to the U.S. government that Americans are required to do. American governments are always complaining about jobs lost overseas, but turn a blind eye to the jobs that exist overseas that Americans aren't considered for because of U.S. government policies. The U.S. plays a great game of preaching globalization but conveniently ignores the fact that it should also apply to the labor force. Particularly the American labor force.

The U.S. government claimed their policies were for security and tax evasion. However, over the years, none of their efforts stopped terrorist funding, tax evaders or drug smugglers. They only compromised the ability of ordinary Americans to get jobs around the world like everyone else and made it expensive for Americans to retire in otherwise overseas cheap retirement communities, just because of the exorbitant accounting and legal fees they'd have to pay for all the paper work to keep Uncle Sam satisfied.

Meanwhile, American companies wanted to appear to be politically correct and friends of the world by hiring foreigners. On the contrary, foreign companies and governments took care of their own nationals.

I quickly gulped down my non-alcoholic beer.

"*Une autre?*" the bar lady asked. "Another?"

"*Non,*" I replied and quickly left before someone came up to the bar and insisted on buying me a "real" drink. I was not inclined to make friends while wearing blue suede shoes.

*Chapter Twenty Seven*
# Saül and Saxophones

After I settled back into Cayenne, I got a call from Michele who indicated that she learned of a U.S. World War II bomber that went down near the village of Saül in the southern part of the country. She didn't think it was Larry's bomber but thought that I might learn something by talking with the villagers there.

I agreed.

In the meantime, I called my contact at Maxwell Air Force base in Alabama that kept files of the Missing Aircrew Reports. I explained I was in French Guiana and gave him enough details of the aircraft to find something in their files and fax them to me in Cayenne.

Michele set up a flight with a private bush pilot named Cisco. He flew a single-engine Cessna and mostly serviced mining stations around the country. He typically got paid in raw gold nuggets and showed me a jar of them from his last flight. He appeared to be about eighty years old but had the spry step of an eighteen-year-old and when he heard I flew down from Chicago, claimed he was related to the famous Cermak family there. I never heard of the family, but there was a Cermak Road that I often took to Chicago's Chinatown district. He claimed that it was named after his relatives.

I don't know if it was the same family, but there was an Anton Cermak who was mayor of Chicago in the 1930s. Unfortunately, he was killed by an assassin's bullet meant for U.S. politician Franklin Roosevelt who later became president.

I didn't have any gold nuggets but Cisco also accepted payment in U.S. dollars.

A short flight landed us on a grass airstrip outside of Saül. There was even a small cabin along the field for waiting passengers with a sign out front that said "Saül" as if it were a major airport.

From there, we walked into town, where we met the village elders and others familiar with the crash site.

The most prominent building in Saül was the church, so I assumed the town was founded by missionaries. Aside from the church, there was little else but low rise bungalows where the locals lived and a small wooden house labeled with a handwritten sign that said "Casino." However, I learned that the town was originally set up by gold prospectors. The church came later.

"Yes, there was a big plane crash here," one of the elders explained. "We heard a big boom in the sky, then saw the plane crashing to the ground. But nobody survived. We buried them near the crash site."

"Is the airplane still there?" I asked.

This triggered a heated conversation in a local dialect.

"I am very sorry to say this," the elder continued. "But everything was taken from the airplane. That was the custom here if the people were dead. Someone even made a saxophone from the airplane's aluminum."

"Can I see the saxophone?" I asked.

"He wouldn't like it," the elder said. "Today everyone is very embarrassed about taking the airplane parts and afraid the U.S. government is going to come after them, but at the time, it was the custom."

"So, there is nothing left of the airplane," I persisted.

"There are only the graves where we buried the men," he replied.

This was bad news for me. It meant that any airplane that went down in the jungle here was likely stripped bare, suggesting there might be nothing left of Uncle Larry's plane.

"Can I see the graves?" I inquired.

This triggered another heated discussion in a local dialect between the elder and a younger man.

It was up to the younger man to take me there, but he explained through the elder that the place was very difficult to get to and haunted by spirits.

I got very American about this and asked him what it would cost. He replied that he didn't want my money. He just didn't want to go there. Meanwhile, a young, attractive local girl listening to the conversation put her arms around the young man's shoulders, kissed him on the cheek and taunted him to take us. I assumed that she offered him protection from evil spirits and a bit more.

He relented and took us to a site where we needed to make our way through some muddy ground and duck and dodge our way around prickly bushes, but nothing close to what I had just endured. It wasn't that bad after all.

We found the site.

The locals had respectfully made iron crosses for the men to mark the graves. I took some pictures and we left. The young man continued to decline any money.

We walked back to the grass airfield and waited for Cisco. Then we flew back to Cayenne where a fax was waiting for me at the Novotel from the Maxwell Air

Force base. It was a Missing Aircrew Report for the plane. The report had all the details of the crash and further indicated that the bodies of the airmen had been exhumed and repatriated back to the U.S.

At least some families got closure.

## Chapter Twenty Eight
# Devil's Island

I had several days left in French Guiana before catching my flight back to the U.S. and wanted to make the most of it.

Devil's Island was on the top of my list.

I had seen the movie *Papillon* with Steve McQueen and Dustin Hoffman and it captured my imagination. Dustin Hoffman played the famous French counterfeiter, Louis Dega, while Steve McQueen played the part of safe cracker Henri Charrière who was convicted of murder but denied the charges and became the friend and protector of Dega in the film.

Devil's Island is one of three islands forming the *Îles du Salut* or "Salvation Islands" group, about nine miles off the coast of French Guiana. The other two are Royal Island and Saint Joseph Island. They were originally considered healthy places for mainland French colonials to take respite from mosquitoes and tropical diseases.

The islands started to become settled in the late eighteenth century, when they were used by ships supplying colonies on the mainland. They were very useful in this role. The Cayenne capital was difficult to supply with freighters because the nearby river was frequently silted so the islands provided a good point for unloading cargo. Later, the islands were used to house soldiers protecting the coast.

Towards the end of the eighteenth century, the idea of deporting convicts and political prisoners to the islands took hold. The French were looking to colonize Guiana, or Guyane as they called it, as well as take pressure off of over-crowded prisons in France. Subsequently, they looked to the British experience of deporting convicts to Australia and sought to apply the same formula.

But once you finished your jail term there, you were expected to spend an equal term living there as a "free man."

However, inadequate planning and infrastructure led to the failure of this experiment, and the islands primarily became the domain of serious offenders and political prisoners. The Alfred Dreyfus affair, being the most noteworthy. Dreyfus was an artillery officer accused of passing secrets on to the Germans and sent to the penal colonies of French Guiana. However, when the real spy was found the government was totally embarrassed about it and sent the spy off to Tunisia to cover things up and presumably shut him up. However, when the public eventually found out about the Dreyfus cover-up, there was a huge out-cry. He was re-instated into the military and received an official apology. Since Dreyfus was Jewish in Catholic France, many accused the government of anti-Semitism and racism in its actions. I don't know what happened to the real spy sent off to Tunisia.

The largest island, Royal Island, *Île Royale*, was the seat of administration and home for prison officials and their families. Trusted prisoners also lived on the island where they plied trades in support of the island's needs and worked as domestic servants.

A church offered prisoners respite from the daily drudgery and prisoners etched frescoes on church walls under the direction of the famous French art forger Frederic La Grange.

Saint Joseph Island, also known as *Île Saint-Joseph*, was where prisoners were sent for solitary confinement. Ironically in more recent times, it has been sought out by boaters, looking for seclusion.

Devil's Island, also known as *Île du Diable* was reserved for political prisoners, who lived in small houses rather than cells, and were relatively unsupervised compared to other prisoners.

The island is across a relatively narrow channel from Royal Island, but strong currents and sharks made it fairly secure. In fact, prison wardens were even cautious about crossing the channel by boat and typically supplied the island by wire cable.

The penitentiary was closed in 1953 and in recent times the islands are being developed as a tourist attraction.

They are accessible by ferry from Kourou.

*Chapter Twenty Nine*
# Music

Throughout most of my travels, I was inspired and often saved by music.

Typically, I traveled alone, and often a single song popped up on the car radio or in a bar that inspired me. It became my best friend and traveling companion for that particular journey.

The song magically appeared when I was lonely or had doubts about what I was doing or surviving the mission. It raised my spirits and gave me the energy and commitment to carry on.

When I first arrived in Cayenne, French Guiana, I was committed to the mission but unsure about what I was getting into. This was slightly different from the various war zones I had jumped into during in the past, where I planned the mission, didn't trust anyone, hired and fired people on the ground and tried to manage my risks. The difference here was that I was giving up control and going into a forbidding jungle where I had few skills with people I had never met before. However, as noted before, one song kept coming up on the car radio which inspired me to keep going. In this case, it was both the song and the lyrics.

It was sung in French Creole in a musical style known as *zouk*.

I find it hard to translate the word *zouk*. It is often translated as "party" and is typically associated with

Caribbean spontaneous "Jump Up" street parties. But it has its own unique, sensual style that defies words. It is typically sung in French or French Creole which adds to its attraction and romance. It is not dancing music like rock or disco, but motivates you to jump and jive in place to the beat. You feel like jivin' even if you're sitting in a chair behind a desk. First your shoulders start twitching, then your waist. Next your head bobs back and forth, then side to side.

Creole was a language spoken between colonials and natives in various parts of the world. Neither side could be bothered to learn the complexities of each other's languages so they created a simplified communication system.

It was often called a *pidgin* language, but this is not correct.

*Pidgin* is typically a collection of ad hoc phrases devised to get a job done or give directions and descriptions to workers, but not a real language. It is more like "baby-talk."

Perhaps, the most widely known pidgin phrase was that used by the British in Hong Kong and China, *chop chop,* meaning "hurry up" or "do it as soon as possible."

On the contrary, Creole is an adaptation of the mother language. It has structure and grammar but in a simplified form. The French version established itself throughout much of the Caribbean and the southern U.S., not just as a language but also as a culture and cuisine. Most notably in New Orleans.

I searched all over Cayenne for this song but because of my incompetence in French couldn't find it and remembered only the reprise.

*Ce n'est pas difficile.* "It's not difficult."

I sung it in it record shops but they couldn't help me. Then the Novotel hotel got the phone number for a local radio station and I sung it over the phone for one of the DJs.

He came to my rescue.

It was called *Ou Piraté Mwen* and sung by an artist called Peggy. It was the reprise "it's not difficult" that inspired me to continue the project and endure the hardships of the jungle.

I later learned that the title meant "You took possession of my body and soul."

Given my years of obsessively searching for Larry, I began to think that's what he did to me.

*Chapter Thirty*
# Cosmic Commitment

One morning shortly after returning home to Chicago from French Guiana, I woke up with chills and an incredibly high fever.

It was summer but I was shaking all over and could barely make it to my doctor's office, which was only a short taxi ride from my apartment. My doctor didn't know what was wrong with me. Maybe the British SAS were right and I shouldn't have taken that bath in a French Guiana creek after all.

My doctor tested me for not only the obvious such as malaria, but everything else he could think of, yet all the results were negative. The best he could offer was a cocktail of drugs and the suggestion that I take a warm shower, which he said would relieve the chills and the pain of the fever.

"Are you sure a warm shower is okay?" I asked. "I suffered from high fevers as a kid and my parents' reaction was to put me in a very, very cold bath, which was very painful but brought my temperature down."

"I don't believe in torturing my patients," he replied. "A lukewarm shower should work."

The warm shower actually gave some relief. But most days I was wrapped up in blankets and shivering and sweating underneath. And leaving those blankets to run into a shower was painful in itself.

In the meantime, in the middle of shivers, I contacted Ted Kaufman.

I didn't tell him that I had been to South America or that I was sick. I only told him that I had better maps of the area and asked if he would do another dowsing.

He agreed.

The maps I sent had no coordinates. They were photocopies of sections from the French topographic maps. I was still cynical and testing his methods.

A week went by and I didn't hear back, so I called. I got his wife.

"Oh, Peter. Thanks for your call," she responded cheerfully. "Ted got your maps but fell down coming back from the mail box and broke his hip. But don't worry. He knows how important this is to your family and is working on it in the hospital."

I was stunned. This whole project seemed to be jinxed by "powerful forces" as indicated by the psychic. Obviously, they were evil forces. My grandmother died shortly after she gave me information about Larry. I twisted my back training for the jungle. Then the psychic got scared and I came back from the jungle with a fever no one could explain. Now Ted Kaufmann falls down and breaks his hip after getting my maps.

The last thing I ever wanted to do in my life was go back to French Guiana and repeat the jungle experience crawling up and down muddy hills, sweating from the heat during the day and freezing from the damp cold at night.

However, one night during a high fever I made a pact with the Cosmos. The terms were very simple. So I thought. If my fever breaks, and Ted Kaufman marks an X on the new topographical maps and that X is close to the one he did before, I will go back. The maps had no latitude or longitude markings, so there was no way he would know what area he was dowsing.

My fever broke one week later and I called his house.

When I called, his wife answered the phone again.

"Hi, this is Peter Boczar in Chicago," I explained. "I was checking to see if Ted is out of the hospital yet, and if he made any progress on the maps I sent him."

"Oh, I'm really sorry," she replied. "His hands were shaking really badly from the medicine they gave him. He knew how important this was to your family and kept trying, but one day while he was trying to get a fix on your map, he died."

"He died?" I asked, stunned by what I just heard.

"Yes, I'm really sorry," she replied. "He died."

"No. I'm really sorry," I returned. "I am so, so sorry."

There was nothing more to say and we exchanged sad farewells. The scary thing was that it seemed Kaufman had died the day that my fever broke, almost as if the Cosmos needed to exchange one life for another to keep the Universe in balance.

Now, it was my turn. I had made a deal with the Cosmos and was under pressure to go back to French Guiana, even though the idea of it scared the living daylights out of me. Kaufman had not come up with a new X, so the terms of the contract with the Cosmos were not completely fulfilled. Technically, I could have gotten out of it. However, I felt I was obligated to acknowledge his sacrifice. For me, it was a point of honor. He did more than I could have ever asked of him.

He died trying.

*Chapter Thirty One*
# French Guiana Part II

In my mind, I didn't want to get out it of. I cut my deal with the Cosmos and they betrayed me. The Cosmos sacrificed Kaufman for daring to help me in my quest. I needed to challenge that dare. I was angry and the Cosmos needed to be put on record for this.

I called up Michele in Cayenne and said I wanted to plan another trip. We were approaching the end of the weather window, so I had to move quickly. I told her I wanted the same team and we'd follow the same path, but needed more time to get to our objective and a bigger team to carry supplies.

On the first trip, I felt I needed to carry my own gear. But then I learned that most of the famous jungle explorers, known for their African expeditions, had teams of porters carrying their equipment and setting up nice camps for them at night. They didn't even carry their own rifles. So I felt no shame in hiring porters. I was management, not muscle.

She called me a week later.

"I have some news for you," she explained. "But it is complicated. Stephane is willing to go again, but Pierre is not available. Also, I found two extra guys that can go along to help carry stuff. One is called Keno. He is from Suriname and goes into the jungle all the time for mining companies. He is big and strong. The other one is Miguel from Brazil. He grew up in the jungles. He is not so big, but he is an expert hunter and can help you find something to eat in the forest if you get stuck."

"Perfect," I said. "So what's the complication?"

"As before, the government needs you to take one of their people along. Last time it was Pierre, but this time it's a girl."

I'll call this girl Valerie, not her real name.

"Not a problem," I answered. "What's her experience?"

"That's the problem. You should talk with Pierre. He recommended her."

"So isn't there someone else?" I questioned.

"There is but there isn't. Everyone is saying that Valerie must go. Talk to Pierre and her boss."

"Give me the phone number for Pierre and her boss," I replied.

I called her boss first.

"Hi, my name is Peter Boczar from Chicago and I wanted to ask you about Valerie, who is assigned to go with us on my research project," I explained.

"Yes, she is very eager to go," the woman replied.

"Yes, but some people question her abilities and in fact ask that you come instead."

"That is impossible," the woman replied. "I am not available."

"Is there anyone else available?" I asked.

"One guy," she replied. "But he is very busy. Also, Valerie is telling everyone you are a sexist American because you have asked questions about taking her."

"I'm not sexist," I replied. "You are a woman and I just told you that I am happy to take you."

"But Valerie is the only one available," she returned.

The conversation ended there.

I called another source.

"She is a problem," he said. "She is very arrogant."

I called Pierre.

"She is fit enough to do it, but I can't speak for her mentality," he replied. "Don't worry about it, my friend, just bring some Viagra and you'll be fine."

That was not reassurance and I was not looking for a jungle romance. My focus was on the mission.

A few days later, Michele called me back. "I'm sorry to tell you but you must take Valerie with you or you can't go."

"What do you mean I can't go?"

"You are going back into the closed area, so we need government permission. Without it, the pilot cannot fly you there. And without Valerie, the government will not approve it.

"Meanwhile, I should let you know that Valerie is telling everyone that you are a sexist, racist American pig because you don't want to take her."

"So, I've heard," I replied.

I said that I'd decide on whether to proceed with the project after I met her in Cayenne.

Weeks later I was back in Cayenne in the lobby of the Novotel.

I asked Michele to set up a meeting with the team several days in advance, so I could explain the project to them, show them the maps and get their input. I wanted them to be part of the plan, listen to my ideas based on my previous experience but get their input. I wanted their reassurance and buy-in.

I couldn't envision doing another trip slipping and sliding up and down hills getting grabbed by prickly bushes and not knowing where we were. It's important to listen to the experts. But experts in any field have their own flaws, egos and agendas, so bottom line you need to take the decision yourself and live or die by it.

According to my plan, we'd follow the previous *topofil,* if it was still intact, to the original base camp, then take the high ground from there to Crique Alina. However, this time we wouldn't go down to the creek. Instead, we'd continue to follow the high ground north along Crique Alina to a spot where it intersected with a secondary but significant creek. This would give us a definite waypoint independent of the GPS and the compass.

In my mind, even if we had to wade up Crique Alina in chest-deep water, it was better than hacking our way through the jungle and at least we'd know where we were going.

Everyone agreed, nodded their heads and gave me confidence that I had a viable plan. Miguel asked about Caimans. His father had been taken by one. Stephane answered honestly indicating there were Caimans in the area. In this regard, he tried to get approval to bring a shotgun along but was denied by the authorities.

Then Valerie showed up. I guess I should have expected her to be late. She made a primadonna entrance wearing short shorts showing off shapely legs and a braless tank top that flaunted tantalizing breasts. She was a pretty girl with long hair and exuded animalistic sex appeal.

But I wasn't sixteen years old, knew a number of women in my time, and all of the above was quickly overruled by her immaturity and arrogance. In my mind, brats have no sex appeal no matter how good they look. While some guys may see hot bodies and gorgeous looks, I see hassles, aggravation and credit card bills. I learned the hard way. They also tend to be self-indulgently late. That's how you know whether they are worthy or not. Anyone late in my book is quickly off my list, I don't care who or how important.

Years ago, a friend had invited me to a cocktail party in Hong Kong featuring visiting British royalty. I expected an agonizing wait before they showed up, but they were precisely on time and made the effort to shake everyone's hands. I was impressed.

I re-explained my plan for Valerie's benefit and she immediately dismissed it with condescending sarcasm.

"We can make that place in one day, if these guys are not too lazy," she asserted, insulting the rest of the team members who were now shaking their heads.

I had no patience for this but was now on the spot and knew I needed to make it work if I was going to complete the mission. My career in advertising taught me to manage diverse personalities and felt I could handle this one.

"Well, Valerie, I appreciate your thoughts, but this is the plan," I explained. "Based on my previous experience, we can't do this trip in one day. Maybe you and the rest of the team can, but I certainly cannot.

"We meet at the airport at seven in the morning day after tomorrow. Anyone not there on time, we go without them."

"Well, it's up to you if you want to waste your time," she answered back and strutted off.

Keno and Miguel looked at each other and shook their heads, then looked to Stephane for sympathy. It was beyond his control and he shrugged.

"Valerie is an arrogant, immature, little brat," I said candidly to the team. "But I was told that if we don't take her, we can't go."

I was trapped. Give up the mission or bring along Valerie. So I reluctantly agreed to take her along and hoped to make the most of it.

*Chapter Thirty Two*
# Back to the Jungle

I had very bad feelings about this trip. The warning of the Chicago psychic, my grandmother dying, me getting sick with an unknown fever, the Cosmic deal, Kaufman dying, and now Valerie.

I asked Stephane to meet me at the hotel for a drink that night. I wanted to be totally honest with him about my thoughts. I told him I had a very bad feeling about this trip and reserved the right to cancel it any time right up to the helicopter insertion in the jungle. I'd still pay everyone for the days we agreed to whether we went or not.

I told him about the famous dowser who put the X on the map as well as the psychic who warned me not to go. But that just intrigued him and he wanted to go even more than before.

"Don't worry," he said encouragingly. "If you don't want to come, we can go without you." He didn't show any trace of any concern or superstition. Stephane was mission oriented and fearless and practical about what he would encounter. He most certainly was the Indiana Jones of French Guiana.

After drinks with Stephane, I went back to my room. I checked and packed my gear for the next morning in case I would be going, then took off my clothes and lie in bed.

I meditated with controlled-breathing exercises, looking for an answer or encouragement or anything.

After a couple of hours, I felt a warm, loving glow come over me that said everything would be okay. Shortly thereafter, I fell asleep and woke up the next morning feeling really good. I shared that feeling with Stephane when I picked him up for the ride out to the airport and told him I now felt good about the trip.

We got to the airport with time to spare, and much to my surprise, everyone was there on time including Valerie. But she forgot her passport and the airport officials wouldn't clear the flight with her onboard without her passport. However, without her onboard, the flight couldn't take off because we were going into the "closed area" and needed to be accompanied by a government representative.

So we hung out while Valerie argued with the airport officials. It was all in French so I couldn't catch what they were saying, but it was obvious that Valerie was used to getting her own way, and seemed to have the upper hand in the matter. Ironically, I hoped she would prevail so we could get on with the mission.

Meanwhile, a local journalist with the national paper took some pictures while the team loaded the back of the helicopter with our gear.

Fortunately for the mission, Valerie got her way and we got permission to take off.

Once again, I got the privileged front seat next to the pilot and the others squashed themselves into the back. As we were flying over the broccoli-covered jungle I turned around and gave Stephane the thumbs up sign to reassure him I was still feeling good about this. He returned the sign, while Valerie was face down trying to avoid air sickness. As I looked out across the fields of broccoli, I saw that there was a heavy mist hanging low over the jungle. I was concerned, but the pilot Martel said he could handle it and there'd be no problem landing.

I looked down into the broccoli below and couldn't believe I was going to do this all over again. At least this time I was better prepared.

I wore my Vietnam jungle boots which had served me well in Haiti as well several war zones. What I really wanted were Thai Army Special Forces boots. Years ago, I had bought some at Bangkok's Sunday market which offered a lot of military surplus gear. They were canvas and like wearing high-ankle basketball sneakers and extremely lightweight. You could run a marathon in them. The only issue I had with them was that the soles were not very strong and didn't protect you against sharp objects. You could feel the ground below you as if you were walking barefoot. Anyway mine no longer fit and I didn't see them in the military equipment catalogues.

I had also brought along a light-weight North Face mountaineer's sleeping bag so I wouldn't freeze during the cold, damp jungle nights. And I didn't bother with gadgets like water-purification pumps. Additionally, I brought two hand-held marine VHF radios that each had five watts of power as our communications link between the ground team and the air team.

Meanwhile, I learned that my GPS device offered an "extended antenna." It was just a long piece of wire that plugged into the unit, but seemed to give it greater sensitivity and range.

I also replaced my leather gloves with "water skiing" gloves that were more padded and hopefully offered more protection. Since they were designed for the water, I assumed that at least they wouldn't rot, like my leather work gloves. I also bought plastic water bottles that I could clip onto my pack and brought a change of clothes, that I'd leave with the hotel. Given the muddy conditions of the jungle, I also bought sandals with clip straps rather than Velcro.

Additionally, I brought a change of socks and underpants for every day so I'd have dry clothes to start the day with.

At the end of the day, the original socks and underwear were so heavy with humidity that I wanted to leave them at the campsites. They were so thick with moisture that I couldn't even burn them in the camp fire. Valerie accused me of being a typical wasteful American for doing so. Stephane noted that they probably wouldn't decay well in the forest because of all their synthetic fibers, so put them into his *tuke* and carried them out.

Martel found the original landing zone with no problem and everyone scurried out.

Stephane, Keno and Miguel repacked my gear with theirs which left me with a very lightweight backpack, carrying only my camera and navigation gear, water and snacks. The loads that they carried on their backs were impressive. They all carried the *tukes* in canvas duffle bags with straps, except Valerie who had a typical camping store frame backpack with padded shoulders and waist bands.

Most of our supplies were pushed into the water-tight *tukes*, but the rest were just carried along in black, heavy-duty, plastic garbage bags that Stephane and the others strapped to their backs. Most of the team wore long-sleeved shirts as protection from the brush and Wellington style rubber boots, except Valerie who wore a light, sleeveless tank top, cut just above her belly button, which she often rolled up to check for leeches and show off her tight tummy.

We agreed that the first day we would make it to the original base camp, settle in and store gear. Valerie insisted on taking charge of the *topofil*.

The lineup was Stephane on point, me next providing navigation, Keno and Miguel carrying very heavy loads with our supplies, then Valerie stringing along the *topofil*. She was singing to herself in French as she walked along. It was very cute and I felt guilty that perhaps I judged her too quickly. I thought that if I was going to die in the jungle, it would be nicer to die in Valerie's arms than Stephane's.

Later events changed my mind.

Much of the *topofil* that we laid down on the previous trip had been broken up by breaking branches, fallen trees or simple decay. But there were enough visible bits and pieces left to reassure us that we were on the right track and we made our way to the original base camp without too much effort. I'm sure my lightened pack had much to do with that perception. Also, my Vietnam jungle books were perfect for the occasion.

We dropped our gear and began to set up camp. Stephane's first job was to string up the plastic tarps that would protect us and the campfire from the tropical downpours that erupted without warning.

My first order of business was to set up my hammock, tying it between two trees, again at least three feet above the ground to make sure I didn't get run over by a pack of wild boars during the night.

It was the end of the dry season, and the nice stream we enjoyed on the previous trip was down to a trickle. So you had to dig a hole into the muddy bottom to fit your water bottle inside to get enough water for drinking, cooking and washing. There was almost as much mud in the bottle as water.

Everything seemed to be going along well, until I heard Valerie hysterically screaming in French. Stephane grabbed the machete and we raced out of the camp expecting to find Valerie being strangled by a boa constrictor.

Instead, Keno and Miguel had found a bigger stream about fifty feet away from the camp and were quietly bathing themselves in it.

Nothing seemed wrong.

"They are destroying the rainforest," she shouted as I arrived with Stephane. "I must report this to Paris."

Apparently, Keno and Miguel had chopped a narrow path through the brush down to the stream from the campsite. Additionally, they chopped down small trees and used the wood to erect a small cabin-like frame to support their tarps and hammocks.

I told Stephane that I was also going to report this incident to Paris, but my report was going to be about Valerie, and not Keno and Miguel.

Stephane said something in French to Valerie which calmed her down and she resigned herself to setting up her camp.

Stephane did a good job of setting up the tarps. No sooner had he finished, it started pouring rain. We all felt cozy and warm underneath the tarps which also protected our camp fire.

Everyone except Valerie.

Valerie was determined to demonstrate her jungle independence and set up her hammock under her own tarp outside the camp, away from everyone else.

While Stephane was cooking up a nice meal on the fire, Valerie was squatting over some pots filled with dried food that needed to be fully saturated with water before she could cook it.

I knew from my own experience that dried food typically needs to sit in water for a long time to absorb enough moisture before you could put it on the stove. Maybe overnight.

I had this immediate horrible vision that our mission and timeline were now held hostage to Valerie's dried food waiting to soak up enough water.

I said to her, "Look Valerie, we have plenty of food for everyone now. Why don't you just come and join us?"

"I don't need your food," she shouted at me. "I know how to live in the forest."

She also criticized Stephane for bringing all the canned food, because it was heavy to carry and not healthy to eat.

I looked at the others and they rolled their eyes.

I thought for a moment, keeping calm, then said. "Valerie, we need to eat our food first, because, as you said, it's very heavy to carry. So, it would be better if you help us eat our food first and we save your food for later."

She accepted that and joined us before the campfire.

After their bath, Keno and Miguel changed into dinner attire. In the case of Keno, it was a Michael Jordan T-shirt, shorts and sandals.

While Stephane was cooking something hot, Keno and Manuel were eating small, dried yellow pellets out of plastic boxes, which they claimed was the secret to their energy and strength. They looked like BBs or tiny beads.

"What's that?" I asked.

Keno said something in French and Valerie translated.

"Tapioca," she said.

Keno offered some for me to try. It was dry and tasteless and I didn't see how they could shovel handfuls into their mouths without a sip of water.

While the evening meal was simmering over the campfire, Stephane prepared his traditional apéritif of *Petite Punch* in the plastic bowls bought from the Chinese "one-dollar shop" in Cayenne.

Valerie initially declined her ration, but Stephane insisted. After a toast, she took a weak sip, then put her bowl on the ground. Keno dumped it into his. No need to let good rum go to waste.

Stephane then broke out tins of sardines in mustard sauce as appetizers with crackers. This was followed by a stew over rice made with canned meat. It was a feast and tasted great.

I was particularly impressed that Stephane could make perfect steamed rice over a campfire. I couldn't even make it in a kitchen with a proper stove.

After the meal, I pulled out my maps and briefed the team on the plan for the next day. Everyone nodded and indicated agreement except Valerie who was silent and slipped back under her tarp.

*Chapter Thirty Three*
# Base Camp Two

As noted, the plan was that we'd go up to the high ground, proceed west to Crique Alina then follow it north. There we'd establish a forward camp, Base Camp Two, as close as possible to our objective before dusk. The next day, we'd push hard and move fast to the X with day packs and minimal gear.

However, this time we'd stay on the east side of Crique Alina, which offered high ground and lighter jungle and follow it to the intersection with the secondary creek that would give us a reliable waypoint. Then start our search from there. At least we'd know where we were.

I was up early the next morning due to the noisy insects and my inability to sleep comfortably in a hammock despite all the advice I got about the right technique.

As Stephane was preparing the campfire, Keno and Miguel were repacking the *tukes* with lightness in mind and the assumption that we'd only be gone for at most two nights. Everything left behind was packed into a single *tuke*, then strung up high in one of the trees to keep animals from getting at it.

After a breakfast of hot tea with brown sugar, Laughing Cow cheese wedges and crackers, we packed up and moved out.

We climbed to the top of the hill, took a compass bearing and, hopefully, started heading West. We quickly reached Crique Alina.

As noted, instead of immediately descending down into the creek, we stayed on the high ground along the east bank and followed it north. Crique Alina was always in sight, so we didn't need to rely on compass or GPS readings and always knew we were on course. Also, the route along the hilltop was much more forgiving. The brush was not as dense and we could pretty much stroll along at our own pace.

I also noted my experience from the previous journey that when crossed the creek we got bogged down in thick vegetation and tall razor grass. So I wanted to avoid that as much as possible.

We were making good progress but moving too fast. Everyone was widely separated. Stephane was way out in front and the rest of the team lagged behind. But they carried the loads while Valerie took her time with the *topofil*.

Suddenly, I caught up with Stephane. He had abruptly come to a stop and was transfixed by something in front of him. As I inched closer, I noted that he had stumbled into a huge swarm of bees buzzing around their nest in a tree. He was maybe twelve inches away from them. I was inclined to take a picture, but better instincts prevailed. I was afraid that the flash might go off and send the bees into a frenzy.

Stephane put up his hand signaling me to back away. He didn't even want to speak. Then he very slowly, inched his way backwards trying to stay in the shadow of the jungle. If he crossed into the light, the change in the pattern of light and dark might signal the bees that they had an intruder and incite an attack. I understood that's how insect vision worked.

Stephane was able to back out without incident and we moved on.

We continued to make good progress, then ran out of high ground. We had not yet spotted the small creek to the west, but the ground to the north started rapidly sloping downwards into dense vegetation. So the decision was to keeping heading north, climb down the hill through thick vegetation hacking our way through the bush or cross over Crique Alina onto the west bank. I felt it was better to cross the creek. In retrospect, I should have followed down the hill to the secondary creek even through it was going to be hard going.

As soon as I announced the decision to cross Crique Alina and set up Base Camp Two there, Valerie was ecstatic.

She dropped the *topofil*, then slid down the hillside and jumped into the water.

Everyone else quickly raced down the hill, leaving me behind. I took a slower, more cautious approach knowing that something as simple as a sprained ankle could jeopardize the whole project. We crossed the creek and set up a comfortable base camp on the other side.

The vegetation was not very dense and everyone appreciated the water supply from Crique Alina. Although we were at the end of the dry season, the creek was still full and we had more than enough water for cooking and bathing. Also, the jungle had thinned out there.

We had a relaxed meal in front of the campfire and everyone got a good night's rest.

*Chapter Thirty Four*
# X Marks the Spot

The next day, we started our usual morning routine with hot tea, crackers and Laughing Cow cheese wedges.

We were going to race to the X that Ted Kaufman had drawn on the map. All indications were that we were very close, so everyone just took light packs and some snacks for lunch.

I wanted to go back across Crique Alina and follow it north until we intersected the other major creek heading east into it. If we just headed north from the west bank, we would lose sight of Crique Alina and there were so many small creeks in the area, we wouldn't know if we got to the right one.

We crossed the creek, but the vegetation was so thick and it was very slow going. Visibility was maybe three feet. Keno took point with the machete and hacked his was through dense bush but we were only making about fifty feet an hour.

So I decided to cross Crique Alina again and head north to look for the secondary creek that would give us our waypoint. I would have to rely on my navigation skills.

After a couple of hours we found a creek that fit the bill. But I wanted to make sure. And there was enough open sky-light to try for a GPS fix.

I waded waist deep out into the creek with Stephane holding the extended wire antenna. As I was watching the satellite map and trying to align the receiver, I noted that there was a large fish swimming around my legs.

"Is this a dangerous fish?" I asked Stephane. It was obviously not a piranha, but I thought it unusual that it was brushing itself up against my legs. Was it cleaning itself or infecting me with poison?

Stephane took a look, then quickly gave me the extended antenna and rushed out of the water. He shouted something at the team on the shore, and Keno rushed forward with Stephane's machete. Stephane grabbed the machete then rushed back towards me. Meanwhile, Valerie was screaming hysterically.

Of course, it was all in French and I didn't have a clue what they were saying. However, based on the shouts and screams, I assumed the fish was dangerous and started running out of the creek holding the GPS above my head, trying not to get it wet nor lose my footing and fall into the stream, ruining the electronics.

Stephane ran to the place I had been standing and slashed the water a few times with his machete while Valerie continued screaming.

He came back empty handed.

"So, that fish was very dangerous?" I asked Stephane.

"No. But it is very good eating and would be a very good dinner tonight," he replied.

"So what was Valerie screaming about?" I asked.

"She claimed it was an endangered species and she would report me to Paris if I killed it," he laughed.

I lost it and faced off with Valerie.

"What the hell is wrong with you?" I screamed at her. "I spend all this time and money to come down here for my family, and all you care about is some fucking fish."

She didn't respond.

I was ready to string her up to a tree and leave her for the insects.

Fortunately, before all the drama started, I was able to fix our latitude and longitude from the GPS unit and set a compass course. Unfortunately, I was so rattled by this latest Valerie incident that when I accounted for magnetic deviation I set it in the wrong direction. I subtracted the deviation twice instead of adding it once. Or vice-versa. Quite frankly, I was so upset, I might have added or subtracted it ten times. I should have asked Stephane to double-check my calculations but hindsight is fifty-fifty.

After hiking for a while, I realized something was amiss. The topography of the ground we were covering was not the same as that indicated on the map. I realized my error and tried for another GPS fix. Fortunately, I got one before we lost too much time but had to correct our position twice.

*Chapter Thirty Five*

# A Hole in the Jungle

To get us back on track, I set a course due north and was able to get another GPS fix after a while to indicate whether we were proceeding in the right direction.

Shortly thereafter, I got another fix which indicated that we were closing in on our objective.

During the day's hike, only me and Stephane knew where we were going. Or not, as the case may be. I briefed the team in the morning on our route, but didn't provide everyone with minute-by-minute updates. It would be counterproductive.

Meanwhile, Miguel indicated that he hoped we got lost so he could demonstrate his jungle skills and teach us how to hunt in the forest.

He pointed out a nearby tree that was good for making bows and arrows, and that we could hunt *maïpouri* for food. He'd get us to the major river that fed Crique Alina, chop down a tree and make a dug-out canoe which we could paddle to a village, then get a boat back to Cayenne.

That gave me some reassurance we could get home without the helicopter, but I wondered what Valerie might think about him chopping down trees and hunting game.

"What is a *maïpouri?*" I asked Stephane.

"It is a kind of wild pig," he explained. "It has a long nose and looks like a wild boar but has no tusks. It is very good eating."

After a while, the topography changed again. We crossed a small stream and from the topographical map, I knew that we overshot the X. A GPS fix confirmed it. We were also slightly east of the mark.

So we turned south and slightly west.

At that point, Stephane and I started plotting our way tree-to-tree. That is, you stand with your back to a tree and look for another tree a short walk away that matches the compass heading. Then you walk to that tree and repeat the process. That way, you stay on your compass line and don't wander about trying to figure out how far off track you are once you start dodging the brush in between.

Suddenly, Miguel called out from behind. "That's the place," he shouted.

When I asked how he could be so sure, he replied, "Because there's a hole in the jungle there."

He pointed to a tall, stout, black, telephone pole-like tree that was totally out of place compared with the rest of the vegetation. He explained that tree only grows where there is a "hole" in the jungle, because it needs a lot of space to breathe. He went on to say that this area must have had a big fire or been cleared by people. That's what created the hole, he explained.

A GPS fix indicated we were virtually on top of our objective. I cut a cross on the tree with a knife to mark the spot. But it was a dark, gloomy and swampy place. It felt evil and I didn't believe Uncle Larry died here.

Fortunately, the area to the west of it pointed towards X'. It also opened up into a valley of sorts with lighter vegetation that had, in fact, suggested someone or something had indeed cleared out this space, per Miguel. So that encouraged us to proceed in that direction.

I suggested that I go to the top of the hill south of us, try to get a satellite fix and confirm our position. Then we'd proceed west towards X'. Keno volunteered to go with me.

When we got to the top of the hill, Keno cut a long stick from the brush and we put the end of the wire GPS antenna on it. Then he raised it as high as he could to get better reception.

As I monitored the GPS unit for satellite locations, I directed Keno to move the pole a bit one way or another to pick up the signal. Sometimes it was only a matter of inches to get a satellite fix. I needed three satellites to get a fix and sometimes when I locked in one or two I lost the third. Also, there were not that many satellites in the area.

Keno called it, "fishing for satellites."

After a bit of fishing, I finally got a bite and reeled in three satellites on the screen. I quickly fixed the coordinates before one of them disappeared. They confirmed that we were in the right area, so we started back down the hill to join the others. Keno took the lead.

As we were making our way down the hill, Keno suddenly stopped dead in his tracks and raised his arm, military fashion with his hand upright in a fist, signaling me to stop.

*"Qu'est-ce que c'est?"* I asked in the best of my college French. "What is it?"

*"Un serpent,"* he replied. "A snake."

*"Et-il dangereux?"* I continued. "Is it dangerous?"

*"Très dangereux,"* he replied. "Very dangerous."

Despite his signal to stop, I slowly inched my way forward to get a look at this dangerous snake.

I expected a huge python-like monster, or something with a rattle or a cobra-like hood.

Instead, it was a little, skinny black thing. However, it was up on its hind "legs" and looked ready to strike.

Keno and I backed away and found another path down the mountain.

Unfortunately, he made the mistake of telling the others about it.

"We must find it," Valerie shouted. "It could be an endangered species."

She then ran up the path we just descended.

Shortly thereafter, we heard Valerie screaming and saw the snake coming out of the brush. She was chasing it and throwing stones at it.

"So, Valerie," I asked sarcastically. "What kind of snake was it? Is it an endangered species?"

Before she could answer, Keno spoke up.

"There are only two kinds of snakes in this forest," Keno replied. "The kind you shoot from far away with a shotgun and the kind you chop off the head with your machete."

"And this one?" I persisted.

"The kind you shoot with a shotgun," he answered.

Everyone was fed up with Valerie's antics.

Fortunately, the snake got away and we could proceed with the task at hand, sweeping west along the valley and within the "hole in the jungle."

"Don't expect to find an airplane," Stephane said as we were walking. "The natives would have taken everything."

I heard this in Saül. However, I had seen many pictures of complete airplanes that crashed in the jungle, so held out hope.

"The best we can find are the engines, because they would be too big and heavy to move. But they will most likely be covered with mud."

I kicked myself. I should have noted this from my previous trip to Saül. Despite my meticulous planning, I neglected to bring shovels. I expected the plane to be sitting on the ground.

As we walked along, Stephane stopped whenever he encountered a large mound and poked his machete into it to see if there was anything underneath. Near one of the mounds, I found what was either a wine bottle or a water bottle. It was obviously very old because it had a deep fluted bottom. It looked like the glass bottle was hand blown.

This proved Miguel's theory that someone had been here.

After we reached X', I suggested we could turn back. Stephane said we had enough time to keep looking. However, at that point I felt that if we were meant to find the plane, we'd find it. Nevertheless, I was compelled to leave a token of my uncle's sacrifice and told Stephane I wanted to make a cross with Uncle Larry's name on it.

But I wanted to leave it on a sunny spot on the hill, not in the valley. He agreed that it would be a nice gesture.

He explained to the others and we found a sunny spot on top of the northern slope. However, as Keno started chopping wood to make a cross, Valerie objected that we were destroying the rainforest. Fortunately, Stephane calmed her down and kept her away from me. I never ceased to be impressed by her self-centered insensitivity and immaturity.

I crudely scratched out Larry's family name "Grasha" with the awl of my Swiss Army knife, then colored in the scratches with a ballpoint pen. I stitched the two sticks together with some cord to make a cross, dug a small hole in the ground with my hands, planted the cross and offered a brief prayer.

"Okay, now we can go," I said to everyone.

*Chapter Thirty Six*
# Birds and Bees

I suggested we head directly east to Crique Alina, then follow it south to our base camp.

Everyone agreed except Valerie.

"We need to go back the way we came so we can take down the *topofil*," she explained. "Otherwise, low-flying birds might trip over it and die."

I couldn't believe this, but remained calm.

"Valerie. You saw the *topofil* from the last trip," I countered. "Did you see any dead birds?"

"I insist," she shouted back. "Or I must inform Paris."

Everyone was in disbelief as they watched Valerie trying to disentangle the thread from the brush and roll it up into a neat ball. It would take forever.

Finally, Keno and Miguel exchanged a few words and charged off angrily. I ran after them hoping to calm them down. In the process, I ran into a bunch of bees.

I was stung maybe eight times in the arms and legs. Fortunately, not on the face. When I heard the buzzing, I instinctively put up my arms to protect myself and clapped my hands in front of me to try and squash them.

On the good side, that stopped everyone in their tracks.

"Valerie, give me a cigarette," I shouted back at her.

She lit one of her Gauloises and offered it to me.

It was not hard to find the bee stings. The pain easily marked them.

On the previous trip, Stephane had instructed me that if I am stung by a bee, I should quickly put a cigarette close to the skin to neutralize the toxin with its heat. But at the time, I felt that was too subtle and wanted to be thorough about it.

One by one, I took the cigarette and burned the flesh over the stings on my arms. I could tolerate the pain of burned flesh more than that of the bee stings.

Then I dropped my pants and was about to sit down on a nearby log to work on my legs. I noted that there was a dead bee there. If was more of a wasp than a bee, but it gave me great satisfaction knowing I got one. I quickly took a picture of it. But later regretted that I didn't bring it back home and encase it in plastic as a desktop trophy.

However, I then noticed that there was also a small scorpion on the log and he wasn't dead. So I worked on my legs standing up. I should have also brought him back home.

Fortunately, Valerie gave up on rolling up the *topofil* and Keno and Miguel didn't run off. We all made our way back to Base Camp Two as a team.

*Chapter Thirty Seven*
# Base Camp Two Again

Everyone was happy to be back in Base Camp Two, including me.

I grabbed a bar of soap and my evening change of clothes and proceeded to the stream to wash my jungle digs as well as myself in Crique Alina. I was soon joined by the rest of the team with the exception of Valerie who bathed further upstream so we couldn't watch her disrobe. Disappointing, but fair enough.

The guys stripped off their clothes but left their underpants on. I didn't know if this was because of modesty or fear of infection. As noted, I had heard scary stories about insects in streams that will enter your urinary tract through your penis and lay eggs. So, I followed their lead and kept my underpants on. When I got back to camp I took them off and put on my sweat suit for the evening.

Later that afternoon, we heard a small prop airplane coming our way. It was obviously Cisco. I hired him to overfly our projected position on the third day of our hike and check in with us. I had given him a VHF handheld marine band radio and kept one for ourselves. I specifically selected ones that worked off of pop-in batteries instead of an internal battery that relied on a wall charger. I was afraid that the heat and the humidity would deplete the battery charge and of course there'd be no electrical outlet in the jungle to recharge them. I put our radio and the spare batteries in a zip-lock bag, which I then sealed with duct tape.

We dug out our radio and when the plane got closer, we connected with Cisco.

*"Tout va bien,"* Stephane said into the radio. "Everything is fine."

Stephane then navigated the plane to our position using his ears as Doppler radar. When the plan came closer, its engine noise got louder, when it moved away, the engine noise retreated like the sound of a passing train horn. When the plane was directly overhead, Stephane confirmed our position.

At that point, Valerie grabbed the radio from Stephane and said something in French that I didn't catch. Maybe another *"Tout va bien,"* but she obviously wanted to show everyone that she was part of the act.

Then the plane buzzed off.

Valerie took the initiative to build the fire, making sure to pick deadwood from the ground so we couldn't accuse her of destroying the rainforest.

Stephane relaxed with a Gauloises, while Keno and Miguel dug into their tapioca pellets. I made notes in my journal.

When Stephane was satisfied with the fire, he prepared another gourmet jungle meal. Once the food got going, he served the evening's apéritif of *Petit Punch*. Everyone relaxed and forgot their differences of the day.

*Chapter Thirty Eight*
# Back to Base Camp

The next morning we got an early start on our way back to Base Camp.

Although our packs were lighter given all the food we had consumed, overnight rain had made everything more muddy and slippery. Climbing the steep hills through bushes with razor-sharp leaves was especially challenging. I couldn't believe how Stephane, Keno and Miguel managed to do it. They never grabbed anything for support and never slipped or fell. They had backs like bulls and legs like tree trunks.

We got back to Base Camp without incident and proceeded with the evening ritual of setting up the tarps, hanging our hammocks, building a fire and toasting with Stephane's *Petite Punch*.

The next morning, we got back to the LZ and the guys started chopping down wood and building a single shelter for all of our hammocks. Ironically, Valerie enthusiastically joined in cutting down brush and stringing up poles.

"You're not worried about destroying the jungle?" I challenged her.

"This could be a good spot for tourism," she snapped back.

I was not interested in taking the conversation any further and let it go.

But our challenges were not over.

Fire ants.

When we stuck one of the poles into the ground, out marched a parade of fire ants.

*"Merde,"* Stephane said. "Shit!"

"Don't go near them," he added. "Their bite is very painful. We can't stay here if we can't stop them."

Stephane quickly made a fire and boiled some water.

"We must watch where they come out," Stephane explained. "They have a back door for escape. Once we find that, we can trap them. Then it will be safe to stay here."

Sure enough, as soon as Stephane started pouring the boiling water into the hole from our pole, they started streaming out of another hole about three feet away. He then turned the boiling water on to the escape hole and it was quickly over. The fire ants were defeated.

After the shelter was built and all the hammocks strung up, Stephane suggested that we might spend the afternoon hiking to *Pic du Croissant*. This was a great idea. *Pic du Croissant* had been a focal point of mine since I first got the aerial photographs of it.

However, I was exhausted beyond belief. Again, it was not necessarily the march through the jungle, but lack of a good night's sleep. Although I learned the art of sleeping in a hammock, I still had not mastered it. I figured if they found an airplane they would tell me about it.

The following morning, the march back to the landing zone was very straightforward. So, while the others went off sightseeing to *Pic du Croissant*, I stayed behind. I strung up my backpack and jungle boots from one of the poles so spiders and other critters could not crawl into them, then settled into my hammock and quickly dozed off.

I woke up sometime later to the excited chatter of the team coming back to camp. They had a good day out and seemed to be friends again.

After another one of Stephane's gourmet jungle meals, we shared a *Petite Punch* as the sun went down on the rocks near the LZ, which revealed an incredible panoramic view of the night sky. An infinite number of tiny lights burst through the darkness.

It was a nice closure to a tense trek.

*Chapter Thirty Nine*
# Departure

The next morning, everyone tried to dry out their clothes on the hot, sun-baked rocks attached to the LZ.

Miguel had a special towel for attracting the attention of pilots. It was a naked woman with binoculars. Her lower region was masked by pineapples, but her breasts were fully exposed and she wore the sort of cap that wannabe yacht captains might wear.

We heard the chopper coming long before we saw it. Martel called in on the marine VHF I had given him to ensure we were there. We affirmed and he made his approach.

Martel was on time and he found his way in without any air traffic controller this time.

We quickly loaded our gear and were off minutes later.

I invited everyone to a farewell dinner and asked Stephane to pick out the restaurant. He chose a nice place called *Les Amandiers*. "The Almond Trees." However, I told Stephane that I'd be grateful if I could meet him for a drink at La Bodega in advance. I wanted to revisit the place as a local and not a cruise ship passenger.

He agreed. This time, I wore the change of clothes that I had left at the hotel while they washed my jungle garb.

I picked him up and we drove to the bar.

The same buxom barmaid was still tending drinks there and this time I was smart enough to order a beer that was alcoholic. Heineken.

Some of the Legionnaires there knew Stephane and joined us at the bar. It was obvious that he was highly respected within their community. Stephane told them the story of my airplane search and they toasted me for my effort. One suggested that I should propose the search to the commandant of the Legion as a training exercise.

As it turned out, two days later Stephane was going back to the jungle on some project in the southern part of the country. He didn't eat tapioca pellets, so I had no idea where he got all his energy. For me, crawling through the jungle was an extreme exertion, mentally as well as physically. For him, it was routine.

Everyone showed up for dinner except Valerie. Someone said cynically that she was giving a press conference about our trek. I didn't know whether to take that seriously but it would have fit her profile and didn't really care.

I noted that there was *maïpouri* on the menu and was very curious to try it, especially since Miguel said that's what we'd hunt to nourish ourselves in the jungle if we got lost and went into survival mode. I asked the restaurant where they got it and they told me that the hunters brought it in from the jungle. I pressed the restaurant staff for more information and they indicated that in English it was called a "tapir."

The tapir is a boar-like animal but with a long, pig-like snout and without tusks. I assumed the meat would look and taste like pork. But the look, taste and texture was more like lean beef. It was tender and delicious.

I didn't know what to make of this lot, who earned a living by going into the jungle, but was grateful that they did.

Despite the fact that I had not found an airplane on either search, I felt that I had at least tested Ted Kaufman's hypothesis. In recent days, I've pulled up aerial maps of the location on Google Maps and nothing seems to have changed. It is still like looking down into broccoli. An airplane could have been a few feet away from us and we would never have seen it.

I continued my search, but in a different manner, and thought that maybe it was time to test out the other hypothesis that the plane went down in the ocean.

## Chapter Forty
# Sea Search

As noted, Larry's plane disappeared on March 1, 1944. But the search for the airplane was delayed by a debate among the various Army Air Corps airfields in the Caribbean and South America over who had jurisdiction. I assumed no one wanted to take responsibility for a missing airplane if they could not find it. Meanwhile, one source indicated that planes who followed his flight path wanted to turnaround and search for him but were denied permission. I didn't understand that and assumed something suspicious.

Consequently, the search didn't get started until a day after the plane's disappearance because the various organizations were arguing about who had jurisdiction over the search. Unfortunately, barring a miracle, the crew and the aircraft would have been lost by then. Maybe someone wanted them to be lost.

A day might not sound like much, but if the aircraft went down in the sea, it had already sunk to the bottom. If the crew managed to survive and bob around in life vests they were likely already separated from each other and pushed out of the area by ocean currents or dead from exposure to the elements.

If the plane crashed in the jungle, the high-canopied trees would have already enveloped the crash site.

Nevertheless, I hoped to find those records for any clue they might hold. Again I engaged a researcher who specialized in securing government documents from World War II. Several weeks later, he sent me what he found. The records were held at a U.S. Air Force facility in Florida.

According to the records, Trinidad was given jurisdiction over the search, but U.S. Navy planes were sent from Amapa airfield in Brazil and a blimp was launched from Suriname.

Unfortunately, the records only indicated the amount of time spent searching, but not the areas they searched. Also, the only detailed record was from the blimp, which gave the name of the pilot. I tried to locate him but was unsuccessful.

As noted, before I was introduced to Ted Kaufman, I had been planning my own sea search. That seemed the most logical course of action. The plane was supposed to contact Zandery Field in Suriname, its first landfall on the northern coast of South America, but didn't. So I assumed it had gone down at sea and felt that I needed to explore the possibility of an underwater search.

In the process, I learned about side-scan sonar.

Side-scan sonar involved a boat towing a torpedo-like fish that ultimately produced live video pictures of the sea bottom to an onboard computer. It had been successfully used to find wrecks in thousands of feet of water. Given that Larry's plane would have gone down in less than 150 feet of water, I assumed an underwater search would be fairly straightforward.

Naively, I initially thought that I could charter a yacht and scuba team from Trinidad and follow the plane's route to Suriname while using "fish finder" type sonar for anything bulky on the bottom. At that point, I'd go down with the scuba team to investigate.

I was a certified scuba diver, had done a number of decompression dives, and given the plane's projected flight path and the ever shallower waters, I didn't except we'd ever have to dive more than a hundred feet.

So I went back to the Internet and started looking for companies that did underwater searches. Most of them seemed to work for oil companies, so I expected they would not be affordable. However, I thought that if I could put a proposal together, I could try and pitch potential sponsors. I just needed to estimate a budget.

I found a company in Florida that was willing to correspond with me on the matter. However, they indicated that they only provided the side-scan sonar equipment as well as all the technicians that go along with it but their clients typically provided the boat.

"Boat" was something of an understatement. What they really needed was the kind of research vessel you see in the Jacques Cousteau videos. Basically a small ship.

I had no idea how to find one and asked if I could engage them to find one. I assumed that they had worked with many of these ship owners and could just call up a few of them and see who might be available and what they would charge. We agreed on their fee for this and I waited to hear back.

After a few weeks they said they found a suitable vessel in New Orleans. I thought that was a bit far away and asked why they couldn't find something in the Caribbean or even Florida at least. They claimed all those ships were tied up working contracts for oil companies.

When I asked what this would cost, they indicated thirty-thousand dollars a day and I would need to indemnify them against all losses. I asked them about the nature of the losses and they indicated that sometimes they lose their equipment due to rough seas or poor handling by the ship's crew. I asked why they didn't have insurance for that and they claimed that no insurance company would take on the risk. So, I needed to guarantee another $40,000 to pay for any lost equipment.

I further asked them how many days this would take and they indicated that to do a proper sweep of the area, they said they'd need at minimum of six weeks.

I had my budget.

$1.3 million dollars on the low end.

I asked them to send a contract but they didn't respond.

I assumed they thought that because I wasn't an oil company I couldn't come up with the money, so was wasting their time.

*Chapter Forty One*
# Internet

For years, I'd never go to the Internet for answers.

I grew up in a different generation. If you were researching something, you'd first go to your network of friends and colleagues, who'd hopefully introduce you to their network. Then you picked up the phone and started calling people and working your way through their networks and their networks' networks until you got to the right people. Fortunately, in those days, humans answered the phone rather than a computerized menu maze, and they were typically helpful in directing you somewhere else if they could not assist you.

Enter the Internet.

Importantly for me, my company had since transferred me to its Hong Kong office but the Internet allowed me to continue my research, so I didn't feel like I needed to make a decision between my job and my lifelong mission. The reality was that my job kept me so busy that I couldn't really continue my research until I left the firm some years later. At that time, I decided to focus all my attention on Uncle Larry.

A Google search directed me to various sites that provided information and histories of the Army Air Corps during World War II. They were manned by veterans and knowledgeable researchers. They took questions, provided answers and guidance. Additionally, some customers offered to provide customized research to dig up government documents. For a fee, of course, but the fees tended to be nominal.

I immediately engaged one, who advised that there were more documents available besides the Missing Aircrew Report. Specifically, he noted that I should get the Aircraft Record Card which was a log of the airplane's journey through various postings from the factory to the final destination and everywhere in between.

Additionally, I should get the Aircraft Accident Report which might have more information than the Missing Aircrew Report. In fact, it did. It had the addresses of the crews' relatives.

It listed the next of kin and emergency contacts in the following order.

>Corporal Benjamin M. Evans
>Mrs. Mildred C. Evans, (mother)
>Mr. Irving Evans (father)
>151 Columbia Avenue
>Carrargus, New York
>
>First Lieutenant James S. Buchanan
>Mr. James A. Buchanan (father)
>3800 Reed Avenue,
>Cheyenne, Wyoming
>
>Staff Sergeant Lawrence Grasha
>Mrs. Mary Grasha (mother)
>109 Orchard Road,
>Maplewood, New Jersey
>
>Staff Sergeant Elden D. Hunter Jr.
>Mrs. Florence Benny Hunter (mother)

Edisto Island, South Carolina

<u>Second Lieutenant John F. Healy</u>
Mrs Ruby Hermsmeier (mother)
523 West Pleasant,
Freeport, Illinois

<u>Second Lieutenant Victor R. Harmon</u>
Mrs. Clara M. Harmon (mother)
Rural Free Delivery #1,
Lexington, South Carolina

<u>Corporal Louis J. Enderle</u>
Mrs. Lois Enderle (wife)
c/o Sumner Waite
New Lisbon, Wisconsin

<u>Sergeant Don L. Maheno</u>
Fr. Felton Ward (friend)
Pulaski, Georgia

Mrs. Margaret D. Maheno (wife)
303 East 65th Street
New York, New York

In the meantime, I set up a webpage www.b24search.net which provided a synopsis of the missing airplane details as well as my two searches in French Guiana. I was hoping that people doing their own searches for missing aircraft might come across it and offer their own insights.

I also hoped that my uncle or anyone who knew him might find the website and contact me.

Separately, friends had been encouraging me to post myself on Facebook.

Quite frankly, I didn't know what to do with Facebook at the time. I assumed it was just a site for people to show off pictures of their vacations, children, pets and what they had for dinner. However, I set up an account anyway, but only checked it once a month.

*Chapter Forty Two*
# Patricia

One month that I checked Facebook was very fortuitous.

I got a message from a woman named Patricia Bowen. She claimed she had information about my uncle and wanted to get in touch with me. She found me on the www.armyairforces.com site where I had been posting questions about Larry, his squadron and airplane. She noted that the serial number of the plane I was looking for was the same one that she was looking for. Then she sent me a message on Facebook. Her message read:

> *Dear Mr. Boczar. I have been trying to find a "Peter Boczar" who searched in the jungle for his uncle's missing WW2 plane. My uncle was the pilot of that plane and I hope you are the individual I seek. Your kind response would be very appreciated.*

I replied:

> *Hi Patricia,*
>
> *Thanks for your note. Yes, I am that Peter Boczar. What was your uncle's name? A number of airplanes crashed in that jungle. I am happy to share*

*any information I have. Best to reach me on my email* peterboczar@yahoo.com
*Regards,*
*Peter*

Ironically, although I had specifically made myself visible on the Internet so people could contact me, I was instinctively suspicious now that someone did.

But Patricia was for real. In fact, she was the niece of the pilot of Larry's airplane and like me, she had been conducting her own search hoping to resolve the issue before her father died.

The parallels between her journey and mine were almost too coincidental to be believable. I was the nephew of an uncle trying to resolve the situation before my grandmother died, and she was the niece of the pilot, trying to unravel the mystery before her father died. Also, like my grandmother, her father, grandfather and grandmother had suffered a lifelong sorrow.

Her mission was triggered like mine.

One day, Patricia's father, Robert "Duke" Buchanan, a former captain in the Army Air Forces, gave Patricia his brother's military file, which activated her search.

Just like one day my grandmother gave me the documents she had. It seems that mothers suffer the most from the loss of a missing child and Patricia's grandmother suffered the same lifelong pain as mine.

My grandmother only had letters from the government announcing his disappearance, as well as his letters home, but they had key information such as his Army Air Corps serial number and his last posting, which was Langley Field, Virginia.

That was enough to get a realistic search started.

After we connected on Facebook, we exchanged some emails, then connected on the phone.

Patricia was my spiritual savior. My family was not interested and never supported me on this project. I always felt I was all alone.

Suddenly I didn't feel alone in my search anymore. There was someone I could talk to who considered it as important to them as it was to me.

We immediately exchanged all the data we had retrieved from various sources. As it turned out we both had the same picture of an airplane with the crew in front. She got hers from her family. I got mine from one of the crew relatives I was able to track down, the wife of the a gunner who was living in Jersey City, not far from where I grew up in New Jersey.

However, according to one of the researchers I had engaged, the picture was not that of the plane that went missing. He claimed that it was a B-17, not a B-24 and likely that plane was flying out of Langley Field searching for enemy submarines and not the one on its way to Brazil. Also, the number painted on the front fuselage was 065. H explained that was a "battle number" which allowed pilots to easily identify each other in the sky and not the serial number which would have been on the tail rudders.

The interesting thing was that someone had roughly hand-painted "Daddy of 'Em All" on the front of the fuselage.

"Daddy of 'Em All" is the logo for "Cheyenne Frontier Days," a big annual rodeo and Wild West show in Cheyenne, Wyoming where Patricia and her family grew up. The event goes back over a hundred years and is still running. So, it's likely that particular plane was connected with her uncle.

Her uncle was James Stewart Buchanan. Ironically, some years earlier when I was trying to track down crew members using online telephone directories, I found someone by that name in Wyoming and sent him a letter. Some months later, the letter was returned by the post office as undeliverable.

James "Jimmy" Buchanan was born and raised in Wyoming. He was one of two brothers in the family.

His military files indicate that he was attached to the 309th Bomb Group in June 1943, then Clovis New Mexico, August 1943, then Pueblo Colorado December 1943, then the 6th Heavy Bomb Center, December 1943, Hunting, Kansas January 1944, the 3rd Sea Search Attack Squadron, January to February 1944 in Langley, Virginia where Larry was stationed. Then Presque Isle, Maine.

The last entry confused me, because according to the Aircraft Record Card, the plane departed the U.S. on February 8. Some suggested the Azores. Maybe he was doing a quick delivery there.

However, all subsequent documents listed him as the pilot who flew from Morrison Field, West Palm Beach to Boriquen Field, Puerto Rico, then to Waller Field, Trinidad. Then on March 1, 1944, from Trinidad for Brazil where he never showed up.

In Trinidad, it seemed he filed a maintenance report indicating there were engine problems. Allegedly, Buchanan refused to fly the aircraft given its condition, but he and the crew were marched into a hangar and told that if they didn't fly it then and there, they would all be court-martialed. In retrospect, they should have accepted the court martial. At least, they'd still be alive. In war, it was not uncommon for arrogant idiots in command positions to demand soldiers to take unreasonable actions and threaten them with harsh disciple if they refused.

Buchanan's Aircraft Accident Report indicated that they were assigned to Organization AQ7, Project 90434R whereas Larry's report indicated that they were assigned to Project AQ7A. All very mysterious and to this day, over seventy years later, no one has been able to tell me what Organization or Project AQ7 was.

Patricia was extremely passionate in searching for crews' relatives. She and her husband Carl did a massive road trip throughout the U.S. traveling to nearly every location listed searching for all the crew members' next of kin and any living relatives. She also dug into information about the crew and tried to get to know them as persons through high school yearbooks, press clippings and local library files.

She also researched government archives and military bases to see what she could find. In the process, she waded through a ton of files and bureaucracy. It was a massive effort. More impressive than me going into the jungle.

She also found the sister of another one of the crew members. The brother was a radar mechanic and sent home letters about his overseas transfer about the same time Uncle Larry did. The sister graciously shared those letters with us. He claimed he was on a combat mission and was proud about the rifle assigned to him.

This project also captured the imagination of Patricia's grandson Sawyer Wolker, age eight. I spoke with him briefly on the phone and he said he wanted to go into the jungle like me to look for the airplane. I didn't ask him why, because it would have been an unfair question. When various media asked me this same question, I couldn't answer it. But, like me, I believe the answer would have had something to do with unconditional love for his grandmother Patricia.

Several years ago, Patricia held a memorial service for her uncle, First Lieutenant James "Jimmy" Buchanan in his home state of Wyoming with full military honors. At the service, she paid tribute to all the crew members of that fatal flight.

That was a very beautiful thing to do.

Fortunately, Patricia and I have stayed in touch over the years and she continues to provide spiritual support.

*Chapter Forty Three*

# Mystery Woman

In the midst of all of this, I learned that my mother had a stroke and had to be moved from an assisted living community where she had her own cottage to something more akin to a nursing home for rehabilitation where she shared a room with another person and couldn't leave her bed without assistance.

I made immediate plans to fly from Hong Kong back to the U.S. to visit her in San Diego, California.

I planned to spend a week there and booked a small hotel just down the street from where she was staying, so I could easily drop by and see her.

At first she was happy to see me, but when she learned that I had not moved back to the U.S. and bought a home she could move into with a staff of private servants, she was noticeably less interested in talking with me.

So I had nothing to lose. I broached the unspeakable subject.

Uncle Larry.

"Look, mom," I said. "I know you don't want to talk about this, but I need to ask you about Uncle Larry."

"What about him?" she replied somewhat defensively and looked away.

"Before she died, Grammy told me things that suggested Larry was still alive," I tried to say gently. "Is there anything you can think of, no matter how small, that might give me some ideas?"

"Look, Peter," she shouted aggressively. "Grammy held out hope for her entire life. Everyone held out hope. We kept hearing from people who claimed they saw him in Brazil or Italy or someplace else. It got too painful to hope anymore. It is too painful for me to even think about it.

"You were Grammy's salvation," she continued. "When you were born, Grammy and Pop Pop adopted you as their son."

I then thought that's why Grammy always said I looked like him, but reviewing his pictures, I never saw even a faint resemblance. We were about the same height and weight, had brown hair and blue eyes, but beyond that there was no physical resemblance. I looked more like Pop Pop.

"Sorry, mom," I persisted. "But is there anything else you can remember?"

"I don't want to talk about this," she snapped back angrily. "I told you everything I know. They sent an SOS call that they were crashing in the jungle, then nobody heard from them again."

A chill went down my spine. The Missing Aircrew Report only said the plane was lost over the ocean about sixty miles or less off the northern coast of South America but the radio log was missing from the file. Also, mysteriously the government researchers claimed they couldn't find the radio reports because the plane was no longer attached to a regular military unit but "Organization AQ7." Since he was not assigned to a regular unit at the time, they couldn't help.

"Who told you he crashed in the jungle?" I asked.

"Jean Marsh," my mother answered even more angrily. "Her father went to the Red Cross in New

York and a year later they sent him a letter saying that the plane put out an SOS, that they were crashing in the jungle."

"Who's Jean Marsh?" I asked.

"She was his girlfriend from high school," she shouted back. "That's all I know. It was nice to see you, but I'm very tired, so you can go."

I went back to my hotel.

I continued to visit her the rest of the week but didn't raise the issue of Uncle Larry again.

*Chapter Forty Four*
# Jean Part I

The search for Larry now became the search for Jean.

I immediately returned to the Internet to look for her, but without success. Also, I didn't know if that was her name anymore, but my mother refused to talk about it. The only other bit of information she offered was that eventually Jean got married but her husband died and she couldn't remember her married name.

At that point, I realized I was not going to get anything useful out of her and figured I could continue the conversation on the phone where she might feel less threatened.

When I got back to Hong Kong, I immediately went back online. In addition to doing Google searches based on various key words and telephone directory searches, I signed up for the various ancestor and people search websites.

This led me to various school alumni sites, including the one for the high school where Larry and my mom went to school. Columbia High School in Maplewood, New Jersey. I didn't know if Jean went to school there because in a follow up call with my mom I asked how Larry met Jean and my mom said that they worked together in a department store.

I nervously typed the name Jean Marsh into the school's alumni search site and hit the enter key. Much to my disbelief, her name popped up.

Jean Marsh-Newman-Webb. Class of 1946.

Obviously, she wanted someone to find her.

The site also had an "alumni locater" and indicated that she was living in a town just south of Boston Massachusetts called Yarmouth Port. I immediately went to an online telephone directory and found there was only one Webb listed in that town.

Stanley Webb.

But I hesitated to call. I was shortly leaving for South America to do more research and decided to wait until I got back.

*Chapter Forty Five*
# Suriname

In the process of doing my Internet research, I stumbled across Dave Edhard, a TV producer and director in Suriname whose hobby was the World War II history of Suriname and missing U.S. military aircraft that crashed there.

Apparently, Suriname had supplied eighty percent of the aluminum that built U.S. military aircraft during World War II and provided the U.S. with tremendous support in the war, but was never recognized for their effort. Most people couldn't find it on a map.

I was being very logical about this and looking for companies in Suriname that might have boats and underwater gear such as side-scan sonar that I could hire to conduct a search off the coast.

As noted, Larry's airplane was heading for the Suriname coast and the depths quickly dropped from 150 feet to 30 feet, so I thought this would be very practical.

Dave's name popped up because he had conducted a search for a missing C-54 that exploded and crashed during WWII with thirty-five people on board, including the author of a book called "Lassie Come Home," which later became a popular television series in the U.S. featuring a young boy and his Collie dog.

The plane was en route to North Africa and allegedly carried secret documents and a significant amount of U.S. dollars in cash, presumably to pay the troops.

Dave did extensive research based on government records but only had a vague idea of where the plane might have crashed. Based on that, he interviewed locals in the area who had lived during the period and might have heard stories about the plane crash. The target area was a nightmare. It was a mix of jungle, swamps and rivers.

He then convinced the Suriname military to support him, which they did with helicopters, inflatable boats and men.

The helicopters dropped the team into waist-deep water, and at first they found nothing. But from the air, Dave noticed a tiny island that had unusual vegetation growing on it. It was high and dense. They could see nothing from the air, but he had an intuitive feeling about it. So they went in by boat. Miraculously, the broken-up fuselage of the plane was there on the island.

I also wanted to visit Suriname because Dave had a roster of airplanes that had crashed or went missing. All the aircraft were identified, with the exception of one, which reportedly crashed at a river head called "Shark's Mouth" near the Coppiname national forest.

Dave graciously picked me up at the airport. The flight arrived at night and I was concerned about a taxi taking me to my hotel as a stranger in a strange land.

I had thought about taking a "missing persons" ad out in the local newspaper, but Dave suggested I could get the news coverage I wanted without the expense. The next morning we met in my hotel with a local journalist.

I took Dave and the reporter through the Missing Aircrew Report, provided pictures of my uncle and pointed out his name on the crew list.

Dave and the reporter started muttering to each other in a language that I couldn't identify.

Apparently, they were talking about the surname of one of the crew members. It matched the name of a local family that was originally from the U.S. The father or grandfather had shown up in Suriname just after World War II and became very successful there.

Could this father or grandfather have been a survivor of Larry's airplane?

"How do we find this guy?" I asked excitedly.

"We don't have to," Dave replied. "We know the family. I can call one of them."

At that point, Dave pulled out his mobile phone and dialed a number from his address book. There was an exchange in Dutch and I could tell from Dave's face that the call was not going well.

It seemed the person on the other end was very defensive.

"He doesn't want to talk about it," Dave explained. "He said he doesn't know anything and doesn't want to see you or talk to you."

"Why not?" I persisted.

"He didn't say and just hung up," Dave replied.

Very mysterious.

My lawyers said he had nothing to worry about. They claimed that the statute of limitations regarding any money on the plane had long passed. So even if the father or grandfather retrieved it, they should be okay.

Dave suggested the best thing for me to do right now was to visit the village close to where the unidentified plane went down just off the coast. Unfortunately, he was in the middle of a TV production and couldn't accompany me.

So I asked the hotel to arrange a car with an English-speaking driver. They said they could find me one for the next day.

In the meantime, I wandered around Paramaribo, the capital.

The town was quite charming. It had protected its Dutch heritage and there were many old colonial multi-story wooden homes and shops with balconies within the city center.

At the same time, there were quite a few storefront casinos with Chinese writing on them. Additionally, there appeared to be a number of small Chinese grocery stores and "one-dollar shops." However, their staff weren't as friendly as those in French Guiana.

I entered one grocery store and looked around to see what they stocked. Meanwhile, a girl followed me around the store, presumably to make sure I wasn't going to steal something.

I addressed her in Cantonese, but she didn't respond. I then addressed her in Mandarin, China's national language. No response. I figured I should buy something to show them I was a legitimate customer and not up to anything, so I grabbed a can of Coke and took it to the cashier's counter in the front of the store. I noted the couple behind the counter were speaking a dialect of Chinese that I couldn't identify. I tried saying hello in both Cantonese and Mandarin, but they ignored it. They also had very glum expressions and didn't even look up at me as I spoke. So I just paid and left.

The next morning, the driver came for me.

The first thing I asked was whether he spoke English.

"A little," he replied.

I quickly became very aggravated but knew that losing my temper would not help the situation. This was a typical scam, where a local tourism company sets you up with a guide or driver who doesn't meet your needs, but knows you can't refuse them because you're only there for a short while and don't have time to shop around.

"Where to go?" he asked.

I showed him the village on the map and he seemed to know the place, but he was going to be useless as a translator if I needed one once we got there.

We were headed northwest to a small village along the coast towards the Coppiname nature preserve. It was a pleasant ride along a nice highway. There were road crews all along the highway, but bizarrely, they were all Chinese.

Along the way, we also passed Wong's Supermarket, Choi's Jewelry and several other shops with Chinese names. I learned that the Chinese road crews were from China. When companies from China got awarded projects in Suriname, they brought their own labor. If the workers completed their contract, typically around five years, they might be eligible for a Suriname passport. Additionally, all the Chinese grocery stores seemed to be financed by China with imported Chinese workers. It seemed to be the same global colonization strategy that China employed in Africa.

Of course, once we got to the village, I needed a translator and the driver was useless. So I went to the coast to see what it offered.

There was no sandy beach only soft muddy flats with small young tree saplings and shrubs planted along neat rows in what appeared to be a program to stop erosion. Interestingly, I stumbled across what appeared to be some sort of engine block and a small piston. But obviously not big enough to be part of an airplane. Elsewhere, I noted a piece of sheet metal protruding from the water. Could that be part of a plane?

We drove onward so I could get a better view of the coastline.

Rough, muddy seas crashed in succession well away from the waterfront. I noted that if anyone went down in those waters, it would be a real challenge for them to get ashore.

When I got back to town, Dave met me for a beer. He was disappointed that I was not able to interview anyone in the village. However, I learned from one of my military history researchers that the plane in Shark's Mouth was a fighter and not a bomber. So I didn't feel that I had missed anything. In fact, all of the planes on Dave's missing aircraft roster were fighters with one exception.

My last memory of leaving Suriname was going through security at the airport. There was virtually no customs inspection entering the country, so I was quite surprised by the ordeal when leaving it. There were three security checks. One before immigration, one after and a last one in the departure lounge just before boarding the aircraft.

The last one was the most comprehensive. Everyone, without exception, had their carry-on luggage meticulously searched. The inspector unpacked all of my luggage, threw it on a table then went through the contents item by item.

"What are all these wires for?" he asked aggressively. "Are you making a bomb?"

"They are battery chargers," I explained calmly. "This one is for my phone, this one for my computer and this one for my camera," I politely answered.

"Ok, go," he replied as he haphazardly tossed everything back into my suitcase in a pile. I rearranged my belongings sufficiently to close the suitcase quickly and move on.

I later learned that Suriname was a huge transshipment point for South American drugs headed to the U.S. and Europe. Apparently, they didn't care what came in, only what went out.

*Chapter Forty Six*
# Hugh Van Es

As soon as I got back to Hong Kong, I looked for Hugh van Es at the Foreign Correspondents' Club. The "FCC" as it is colloquially known.

Hugh was a Dutch photographer who covered the Vietnam War and was famous for the shot he took of the evacuation of Saigon. It showed a helicopter precariously balancing itself on some small rooftop structure, while a long row of people lined up along a ladder to the chopper, waiting their turn for evacuation.

His buddies from the 'Nam years called him "Vanes" to distinguish themselves from later less deeply rooted friends. I just called him "van Es." We met a few years after the U.S. departed somewhat unceremoniously from Vietnam.

I first got to know Hugh with a few other friends in the lobby lounge of the Hong Kong Hilton Hotel, which has since been torn down by a property developer for a more profitable investment.

But the magic of the meeting was the appearance of Richard Hughes.

Me and several other friends were in the lounge plotting how to get a friend out of trouble when Richard showed up. Richard was once the Far East correspondent for *The Times* of London, had stomped his way throughout Asia going back to World War II and was generally referred to as "Your Grace." At *The*

*Times*, he had worked for Ian Fleming, who wrote the James Bond novels and based at least one of his characters on Richard.

Richard was always up for a drink and joined our little band to see what we were up to. Maybe something that he'd feature in one of his press columns.

I was the youngest at the table. All the others were veteran correspondents and had at least ten to fifteen years on me.

When Richard heard what was going on, he proposed a toast to me. I would never feel so honored again in my life.

"Young Peter," he said. "As Ian Fleming passed this toast on to me, I now pass it on to you and you may pass it on to anyone else deserving.

"Just remember, young Peter, you are only as good as your friends."

That toast really struck a chord, because growing up I could never rely on my family or friends so I was totally focused on becoming super-independent. At one point, my goal was to join the army and become a Green Beret because in my mind that training made you into someone who could do anything, anywhere, anytime without anybody else to assist you. Because of that toast, I made a point of cultivating friendships and ultimately, did in fact, pass it on to those deserving.

I was eager to find out what the Suriname article said, but it was all in Dutch. So I sought out Hugh and hoped he'd translate it for me. He was also aware of my jungle search and from time to time offered his candid opinion of it, typically in his own very colorful language.

I knew I could find him at his usual spot along the northwest corner of the FCC bar in the evening. He once advised me not to hang out there. He claimed that under the Chinese laws of *Fung Shui,* "Wind and water," it was a bad spot.

"All the dragons coming down from the Peak a the top of Hong Kong island to reach the sea banged their head on the bar columns and create a lot of trouble. Most of the fights at the bar happened at that spot," he noted.

It was bad *feng shui*.

But it was his spot. And Hugh was not someone to be intimidated by a few dragons.

Anyway, I found him there, told him I had just come back from Suriname, made the front page of the national newspaper, but it was in Dutch and asked him if he could tell me what it said.

He looked at it disdainfully, irritated at being taken away from his beer, then proclaimed. "It said you went to Suriname to look for your missing uncle from World War II et cetera, et cetera, et cetera."

Then he offered up some more candid advice. Hugh van Es style.

"Look, Peter," he continued. "How many fuckin' times do I have to fuckin' tell you? If you believe this guy is fuckin' alive, then stop wasting your fuckin' time in the fuckin' jungle. He's not going to be living in the fuckin' jungle."

He then went back to sipping his beer.

He had a point. However, my strategy was to first find the airplane. If Larry's dead body was inside, then end of story. However, if there were no bodies inside, then he might still be alive and I'd stop wasting my time in the fuckin' jungle.

It would be a big relief never to go back to a jungle again.

*Chapter Forty Seven*
# Hong Kong Prediction

I left Hugh at the FCC and started to head home.

My apartment was just a twenty-minute walk along Hollywood Road, but for some reason, I decided to make a detour through Hong Kong's SoHo area.

"SoHo" stood for south of Hollywood Road. It was a restaurant and bar area that expats liked to frequent.

It was always dangerous to walk through SoHo in the evening because, invariably, you ran into someone you knew standing outside one of the bars and could not get past them without joining them for a week's worth of drinks and waking up with a pounding hangover the next morning.

There was something particularly nasty about hangovers in subtropical places like Hong Kong. They consumed your whole body and seemed to last forever. They were known as "three-day full-body hangovers."

I made it through the main street of SoHo unnoticed and was on the home stretch when a friend, Robert, spotted me from a small bar at the very end. He waved me in and offered a drink. He was one of those guys who was notably offended when someone declined a drink with him.

He was with a Chinese couple who I assumed were locals from Hong Kong.

"Hey man," he greeted me, "Haven't seen you forever. Where you been? Let me get you a drink."

I ordered what Robert was sipping, a vodka tonic. When the drink arrived, we toasted and he introduced me to his friends. Then I told him I had just gotten back from South America and gave him the short synopsis of my uncle search.

I proudly said that I had made the front cover of the national daily newspaper in Suriname, but it was all in Dutch and I was looking for someone to translate it for me.

"You know anyone who speaks Dutch?" I asked him.

"Right here," Robert laughed. "This guy grew up in Amsterdam."

That was too weird. Cosmically weird. What were the chances? I asked myself. What prompted me to take the back street through SoHo instead of walking straight home? What were the odds of Robert being there with Dutch-speaking friends at the moment I was looking for a Dutch translator?

His buddy wanted to know more about the story and a number of drinks later, I finished the long version.

"I'd be happy to translate it for you," he replied.

"What would be your fee?" I asked.

"A few drinks here," he answered.

"I appreciate that," I replied. "Let me get it scanned and I will email it to you."

We then exchanged business cards as is the custom in Hong Kong so we could contact each other.

Then his girlfriend, who had been silently listening all this time, spoke up.

"Can I tell you something?" she asked.

"Sure."

"You don't know anything about me, and I don't want to scare you, but I know things," she continued. "And I know you will find what you are looking for in February."

It was the end of January and February was only two days away. I had planned to call the phone number I thought I had for Jean that night, but waited. And because Hong Kong is one day ahead of the U.S. I waited until it was February in Boston.

Then Robert said something ever more creepy.

"I also know things," he said. "And maybe your uncle's spirit has taken over your body, which is why you are so obsessed with this search. Maybe he needs you to find his body, so his spirit can rest in peace."

I immediately thought that the reason I need to find his body is so my spirit can rest in peace.

*Chapter Forty Eight*
# Jean Part II

I waited until it was early evening, February first, U.S. East Coast time and dialed the number.

It rang a few times, then was answered by a man who I assumed was the husband. "Hello, my name is Peter Boczar," I started. "I apologize for bothering you, but I am the son of Josephine Grasha and nephew of Larry Grasha and was trying to get in touch with Jean Marsh who was a friend of my mother's in high school. I got this number from her high school alumni page."

"No bother at all," Stan replied. "I'm her husband and I've heard all about your mother and Larry. I'm sure she would love to speak with you. However, she is very sick, so I'd just ask you not to keep her too long. Let me take the phone to her."

"Hi Peter," Jean replied. "I'm so glad to hear from you. Actually, for many years, I was trying to get in touch with your mother, which is why I posted my name on the Columbia High School alumni site. A number of years ago, I even went to your family's gravesite in New Jersey, to see if your mom's name was on your family's tombstone."

I explained my mother's situation, my search for Larry and how my mother had mentioned her name.

"Your mother feels very bad about it because Larry tried to call home from Florida before he went overseas and nobody answered the phone. Then he called me."

"Did he say anything?" I asked. "I made a promise to my grandmother that I'd find him. I got some military records and made several trips to South America, but still don't have any answers. The only thing I learned was that his plane left Trinidad for Brazil and went missing somewhere along the way."

"When he called me from Florida, he told me he was going to Italy," Jean responded. "But he didn't want his family to know about it until he got there so they wouldn't worry. He said he'd call them from Italy."

"Can I ask you something?" I continued. "My mother said that you received a letter from the Red Cross indicating that the plane crashed in the jungle. Is that correct? Do you still have that letter?"

"Yes, it was from the Red Cross," she replied. "My father went to them in New York City, but we didn't get the letter until maybe a year later. I don't know if I still have it. I gave a lot of things to your mother after I got married. You'll have to ask Stan."

"Sorry Peter, but I need to go to sleep now," she continued. "It is great to hear from you. Call me anytime, but I am not well. I would love to talk to your mother."

Then she gave the phone back to Stan.

"Hi Stan," I said. "Sorry I kept her so long. What is she ill from?"

"She has cancer," Stan replied. "And I don't know how long she is going to last."

I couldn't speak and fought back tears.

I gave Stan my mother's phone number and know that they spoke but neither shared with me what they talked about. However, re-connecting with my mom seemed to give Jean some important closure. So, I felt that made my connection worthwhile.

"How would she feel, if I visited her?" I asked as politely as I could. "Would you be okay with that?"

"I think she would be very happy to see you," he answered. "I think if you came by for a day, it would be fine."

We then exchanged emails and noted I would like to send him some things, including a picture of my uncle with a mystery woman to see if Jean knew who it was as well as a jade pendant for Jean. Jade was supposed to have healing powers.

I told him I'd call and let him know my travel plans in advance and see if it was convenient to visit at that time.

I flew to Boston as soon as possible.

*Chapter Forty Nine*
# Boston and Back

I called Stan to tell him my plans and make sure it was still okay to visit.

"Yes, Jean would love to see you," he indicated. "But you can't stay too long, because she gets tired very quickly. One moment, Jean wants to talk with you."

He then handed the phone to Jean.

"Hi Peter," she answered. "We got the photo you sent and I know who the mystery woman is."

"Great," I replied. "Who is she?"

"She is me," Jean replied with a laugh.

I also laughed and was happy it worked out that way. She was so in love with Larry that I'm sure it would have really hurt her feelings to see him with another girl. I should have thought of that before I her sent the picture.

I flew from Hong Kong to Chicago, then called Stan to reconfirm my visit to Boston.

I had been working in Chicago before my company transferred me to their Hong Kong office and had put a lot of stuff in storage there. I wanted to go through all my storage lockers after I saw Jean to make sure I hadn't overlooked any documents regarding Larry.

I took a flight that got me into Boston early afternoon where I arranged for a car to pick me up, drive me to Jean's house, wait for me, then return me to the airport for a flight back to Chicago.

Jean lived in a lovely home in a nice suburb near Boston. Stan opened the door as we pulled into the driveway and greeted me. The living room reminded me of Grammy's house. It was immaculate and overflowing with knick-knacks.

Stan asked me to wait a moment to see if Jean was awake, then brought me into the bedroom. Jean was in the bed under a thick quilt with only her head showing out of the top. There also appeared to be tubes and wires running from under the blankets to under the bed.

"Hi Jean," I said cheerfully. "Thank you for seeing me."

"Thank you for visiting," she replied.

I didn't feel it appropriate to ask about her condition or how she was feeling. I wanted to ask her about Larry, but was afraid it might upset her. I also noted her examining me carefully, almost as if she expected me to look like him.

"Is it okay to ask you about Larry?" I asked politely.

"Of course," she replied. "I'm happy to tell you everything I know."

I felt it inappropriate to ask about her personal relationship with him, so avoided that subject. Anyway, it wouldn't be relevant to my search.

"Tell me about the letter claiming the plane sent an SOS call," I asked. "Do you still have it?"

"As I told you, my father went to the Red Cross in New York City after Larry was declared missing," she replied. "And they sent him that letter almost one year later. I don't know if I still have it. There is so much stuff in boxes here. Stan has to go through them. We lived just around the corner from your family, so when I got it, I took it to your mother's house. I don't remember if I showed it to your mother or grandmother. Also, after I got married I gave a lot of stuff to your mother including the "wings" Larry gave me.

"Wings" were metal military pins that the soldiers wore on their uniforms to indicate that they were in the Army Air Corps and that they were fit for duty as flight crew. Apparently, depending on your aircraft duties, you wore different wings. Larry's consisted of stylized wings sprouting from both sides of a round shield which indicated he was an enlisted man and not an officer. The interesting thing is that when Larry sent his stuff back to his family the wings he sent were those of a pilot. I assume he was trying to impress his family. In some of his letters he noted that the pilots let him into the cockpit and taught how to fly the plane. He said he wanted to go into aviation after the war.

In pictures of Larry and Jean, Jean was wearing the wings of an aviation cadet. It had stylized wings from the side of a vertical propeller.

"The only thing I kept were his letters to me," she added.

"What was your father's name?" I asked, not knowing why I didn't ask her over the phone. I also asked her the address where she lived in Maplewood, thinking it might help me in my research.

"Frederick," she replied.

"Do you still have his letters?" I continued.

"I don't know, I may have given them to your mother after I got married." she replied.

"Well, I never saw your letters," I replied. "The only letters I saw were the ones Larry wrote to his mother and sister. Was there anything in the letters you think might help me find him or his airplane?"

"Well, he told me he was flying in B-17s," she answered. "So I was surprised when they said he was missing in a B-24. His friends Ray Hugg, Robert Rosetti and Bill Homes said they were going to go to Brazil after the war to look for him. But I don't know what they did and Ray passed away a few years ago."

Jean further indicated that I should take this story to the newspapers and that she would be willing to be interviewed despite her condition.

"Maybe someone will see the story and know something," she added.

I was quite surprised by this. The reason I had not taken this story to the press before was to protect my mother. Given her reluctance to talk about it, the last thing I wanted to do was subject her to media reporters swarming all over her nursing home. But maybe I should have, to force her to tell her version of events. And in retrospect, I'm sure she would have loved the attention.

But now I felt that I had permission from Jean.

"I'm sorry, Peter," she said. "I'm falling asleep right now, but I have all his pictures. Stan can show you."

At that point, we exchanged farewells. She produced the jade pendant I had sent her from Hong Kong. She wanted me to know that she had been wearing it. But obviously it didn't cure cancer.

I kissed her on the forehead and Stan took me into the dining room, where a large photo album was laid out on the dining room table.

It was an amazing collection of photos, not just of Larry, but also of the time Jean spent with my family. She had pictures that my mother and grandmother didn't even have. One was especially touching. It was a picture of her and Larry, but Larry's face was cut out in a heart shape that she fit into a pendant.

Stan invited me to take some, but I didn't feel right about it.

After spending some time with the photo album, I thanked Stan for his understanding and graciousness and caught my flight back to Chicago.

I spent the next day going through every box I had in my Chicago storage lockers marked "documents," hoping to find the Red Cross letter. I had hoped the letter would include the time of the SOS call as well as the position of the aircraft before it crashed. Even if it only included the time of the distress call, I could extrapolate the plane's position based on the details in the Missing Aircrew Report.

I didn't find the letter, but found a yearbook from one of the technical schools that Larry had attended during his training. It was the same one that Grammy had given me years ago. Like most yearbooks, there were a number of signatures in the back. I thought that if I could I identify some of those signatures, I might be able to find their owners and see if they had more information about Larry.

*Chapter Fifty*
# Passing On

A friend in Chicago helped me make some media contacts.

However, I was already back in Hong Kong, so the media interviewed me over the phone in their time zones. I kept my mobile phone on, put it next to my pillow and was often answering questions at four o'clock in the morning. I also put them in touch with Patricia Bowen, who was also interested in talking with the press. Unfortunately, they were not able to get in touch with Jean.

I called Stan after a couple of weeks to see how Jean was doing, but also to see if he had time to look through the storage boxes in their home to see if he could find anything. My mother's health was also at question and I wanted to resolve this before she passed away. So looking through boxes became a matter of life and death.

Stan said he looked through what he thought were the most likely of all the boxes in their house and didn't find anything. But he would keep looking.

"How is Jean doing?" I asked.

"Not good," he replied. "She called for me in the middle of the night and asked me to hold her. I held her all night long and thought I was going to lose her."

"Can I talk with her?" I asked.

"Let me see," he responded. "She can barely speak."

He took the phone to her bedside and put her on the line.

"Hi Jean, it's Peter," I said trying to be upbeat and cheerful.

"Hi Peter," she said weakly. It sounded like she was really struggling just to get out those few words.

"I just called to say it was great meeting you and I wanted to thank you again for all your help," I continued.

"Thank you, Peter," she replied even more weakly.

She then returned to the phone to Stan.

"I'm sorry Peter, but she's very weak right now," he explained.

"No, I'm sorry, Stan, and want to thank you again for your graciousness and help."

Jean died the next day.

Shortly thereafter, my story hit the press, but with no mention of Jean.

Later, Stan sent me all the pictures he had of Jean and Larry including a copy of Larry's high school yearbook.

Stan was a true gentleman.

*Chapter Fifty One*
# Friends & Relatives

The search for Larry now turned into a search for his friends as well as the Red Cross letter.

I initially focused on friends that Jean claimed were going to look for him in South America after the War. Ray Hugg, William "Bill" Holmes and Robert "Rosey" Rosetti. However, since Jean had indicated that Ray passed away a few years earlier, I focused on the latter two. But this was another issue I had with my mother. She could have introduced me to Ray who might have filled in many of the blanks. She could have also introduced me to Jean many years earlier, but did not. She was obviously holding on to some dark secret in my mind.

I first went to the Columbia High School alumni site, but their names did not turn up. I learned that your name wouldn't appear on the site unless you registered it. So I started doing general searches on the Internet. I also started searching for the people whose names appeared on various military sites. But I had no success.

I realized I needed help and decided to hire a private detective but was a little bit reluctant. I only had one previous experience with a private detective. Many years earlier, when I was working at an advertising agency, we sold one of our clients an ad campaign based on some test shots we did with a female model.

The client liked the campaign and was ready to run it just based on the test shots.

However, we had only contracted the model for test shots, so we needed to go back to the modeling agency in New York City and negotiate for additional usage rights. Unfortunately, the agency said that the model had left the company and didn't know how to contact her.

I called up telephone information in New York City, but there was no listing. I shouldn't have been surprised because models often share apartments or live with their boyfriends. Also, she had a generic unisex name like "Bobbi Brown" so there could have been hundreds of listings.

However, we had her Social Security number from the initial agreement and I assumed this would be sufficient in the hands of a trained detective. Many weeks and thousands of dollars later, the detective called me and said that he had found out that she was living in California and had the address.

"How did you find the address? Did you get any photos of her?" I asked.

"I didn't see her, but I know she's living there?" he replied.

"But how?" I persisted.

He was reluctant to divulge trade secrets, but finally relented and said that her mail was going there.

Pictures were important because models tended to age very rapidly based on their lifestyle.

We felt it was a bad idea to send a detective to the house because it would be a bit intimidating, so we sent a TV producer from our California office.

If we hadn't spent so much money on it the result would be comical. I got a call two days later.

"Okay Peter," the producer explained. "I went to the house and a big black guy answered the door. I asked to speak with Bobbi Brown, claiming her modeling agency in New York was trying to get in touch with her. The guy said 'I'm Bobby Brown' at which point I apologized for going to the wrong address and left."

I knew two people who had made a career with the police departments in New York City and New Jersey and contacted them.

One was retired and working as an independent security consultant. However, he said this was not the kind of work he did. I translated that to mean that there wouldn't be enough money in it to make it worthwhile for him.

The second introduced me to someone who said that finding missing persons was his specialty. Mostly criminals on the run. He agreed to a nominal fee assuming it would be easy.

A week later he sent an email asking me to call.

"Well, Peter," he said. "I haven't found this guy yet and I'm way over the fee agreement based on my hourly rate, but I don't have a problem with that. I typically find bad guys who are doing everything they can to disappear, so this is now a personal challenge for me. So, don't worry about it. I'll let you know when I have an update."

A week later he sent me a note with a newspaper clipping dated 1981 with Robert E. Rosetti's obituary. He died at the age of fifty-seven.

The detective suggested that his wife might still be alive and would let me know if he was able to contact her.

I never heard back.

William F. Holmes, son of Fred Holmes, is still missing. I don't know if he is alive or dead. Apparently, the U.S. government has sold its databases to various family search firms that require you to pay a monthly subscription but then make it very difficult to find out anything about anyone. And their data is often incorrect. They didn't even get my mother's birthday right.

*Chapter Fifty Two*
# The Letter

The Red Cross letter, if it existed, continued to be of great importance to me because of the data it might contain.

The Red Cross website indicated that they had document archives going back to World War II, so that got my hopes up.

I contacted the Red Cross in the U.S. and was told that I needed to contact the Red Cross in Europe. I contacted the Red Cross in Europe and was told that I needed to contact the Red Cross in the Caribbean. I contacted the Red Cross in the Caribbean and was told that all their files would have been turned over to the U.S. Red Cross so I needed to contact them.

At that point, I found a professional researcher in the Washington D.C. area who was close to the U.S. Red Cross headquarters. I gave him all the information I thought relevant such as the details of Larry, the name and home address of Jean's father and the estimated time period that the letter was sent.

He got back to me after a week and unfortunately indicated that virtually all the records in the archives were related to Red Cross staff and activities and he did not find any records dealing with individuals outside the organization.

The one thing that held some hope of finding additional information was that the Red Cross in the

Caribbean suggested that I contact the military museum in Trinidad. They said it might have records of all the aircraft that passed through there during the War.

It was a good thought, but when I called, they said that they were primarily a museum and didn't have such records.

Four people claimed that they had read the Red Cross letter which indicated Larry's plane was crashing in the jungle. My grandmother, my mother, his fiancée and her younger sister. This was the most important piece of evidence in the search, but no one could produce the actual letter.

I then contacted the major daily newspaper in Trinidad, the *Trinidad Guardian*, but their archives didn't go back to the 1940s. Another paper *The Beam*, which covered military affairs in Trinidad during the 1940s doesn't seem to exist anymore.

*Chapter Fifty Three*
# Hong Kong Connection

Hong Kong is a big international city that is essentially a small town. It is also a town that many people from around the world visit or live. So on any given day, at any given bar or cocktail party, you could run into anyone. A famous celebrity or just someone from your home town.

And almost everyone is willing to meet with you. I remember years ago meeting Jackie Chan at a cocktail party by coincidence and we had a nice chat. On the contrary, if I were in Los Angeles or New York, some monster of a security guy would have wrestled me to the ground before ever I got near him.

In that regard, I always found Hong Kong to be a magical place.

I also seemed to run into people I knew from all over the world.

I called these chance but meaningful encounters, "cosmic coincidences."

Running into people I knew from the U.S. or who had grown up in my small town in New Jersey were standard fare. However, one evening I experienced one of the most unlikely of coincidences.

I was at a cocktail party after a trade exposition for the local film industry and ran into a movie friend there while trying to get a beer at the bar. He appeared to be with some potential clients, so I didn't want to bother him, but he graciously introduced me to his crowd which included a young guy who was working for him as an intern.

"Peter, tell him the story about your uncle," my friend said.

I gave him the short version. Primarily how a dowser had marked an "X" on a map of South America, which sent me on a jungle adventure in French Guiana.

"My mother probably knows that guy," he said nonchalantly.

"What?" I responded in disbelief. "How so?"

"She is also a dowser and works with the U.S. Association of Dowsers," he explained.

"That's too amazing," I responded. "Do you think it would be possible to contact your mom about it?"

"Sure," he answered. "Give me your card and I'll give you her email.

I was still in disbelief, and didn't really expect him to contact me.

Several days later, he sent me her contact info and an email introduction.

I followed up with her regarding my project and asked if we could set up a time to talk on the phone.

"Sure, I knew Ted Kaufman," she said. "He was quite well-known."

"Well, let me ask you this," I continued. "Would you be willing to do another dowsing for my uncle?"

"I don't do searches for people," she explained. "There are too many dangerous energies involved. They can also harm the person doing the dowsing."

A chill went down my spine. I thought about Kaufman's wife telling me that he died while he was in the hospital trying to get a fix on the topographical map I had sent him.

"But what if you just dowse for the airplane?" I persisted.

"It's the same thing, because there may still be bodies inside the plane," she explained.

"Is there someone you could recommend?" I continued.

"I will have to ask around," she replied. "But I can't promise anything. Most dowsers will not look for people because it is too risky."

We left it at that.

Several weeks later she sent me the contact info for someone who might be willing to do it.

I followed it up with him on the phone, but he didn't sound too enthusiastic. I sent him the same minimal information I gave Kaufman and he got back to me within a week. He also made a mark in French Guiana but it was far away from Kaufman's mark and the plane's projected flight path.

In my mind, Kaufman was the gold standard so I didn't pursue it.

*Chapter Fifty Four*
# Department of Defense

Patricia Bowen sent me a note one day indicating that she had received a letter from a unit of the Department of Defense indicating they were holding a meeting in San Diego, California regarding their on-going efforts to find the remains of missing soldiers and repatriate them.

I wanted to attend, but would have to fly 10,000 miles and fifteen hours to get there for a one-day meeting. Bottom line, I decided to make the trip even though I was not in good health. At least it would be an opportunity to meet Patricia and her husband Carl who had also invested significant time on this project.

This was one of a number of annual meetings held around the country and attended by families who lost relatives in various American conflicts going back to the Civil War.

The meeting was well organized and the presenters very professional. They outlined the goals of the organization and future priorities. Additionally, based on information I gave them about Larry, I found a binder on my table in the meeting room with all the information they were able to pull together at the last minute from a variety of files. After the general meeting there were also one-on-one follow ups with attendees about their specific cases and questions.

But, when they offered a remembrance service for family members to acknowledge and name missing persons, I couldn't speak. It was very simple. They just asked you to name your missing relative. How hard can that be? But I was too emotional about it, and fortunately Patricia jumped in and spoke out on my behalf, "Larry Grasha" she said. I could helicopter into the jungle and risk my life, walk through mud, hack through bushes, but couldn't talk about it or even mention his name.

I began to appreciate my mother's inability to talk about it.

Later, there was also a very efficient follow-up of questions I posed to them during the meeting.

But, obviously, it was a very underfunded organization and could only commit to a few cases a year. They noted that they currently had 78,000 missing in action files from all over the world.

*Chapter Fifty Five*
# Trump Connection

I must say that of all the bizarre coincidences I experienced during the course of this project, I never expected one linked to the 2016 U.S. presidential candidate Donald Trump.

Apparently, Donald's uncle, John Trump was a professor at MIT, the Massachusetts Institute of Technology. During World War II, he had partnered with Larry's airbase, Langley Field, to develop and test super secret high technology projects.

Trump helped develop radar, microwave and magnetic beam projects that had military applications including Gee, Oboe, LORAN, H2X, MEW and SCR584.

Every boater knows that LORAN was a long-range navigational radar system. It was, in essence, the predecessor to GPS. You turned on your LORAN receiver and got two numbers that corresponded to two lines on your ocean chart. The intersection was your position.

H2X was high altitude bombing radar that "looked through" clouds and bad weather to give the bombardier a picture of the ground target. Don't ask me about the others.

When Larry sent a letter home noting he was "going back to school" I assume he was going to learn about these technologies.

As noted, in his last letter home, he said he was on his way to Brazil to test out an "experimental" project devised by a 27 year-old colonel. The commander of his base, Col. William Dolan would have been 37 at that time based on my research, so I don't know if he was referring to him. Maybe it was a typo.

However, magnetic and microwave technologies at the time had as much risk to the users as the targets. So maybe they were a factor in his plane's disappearance.

*Chapter Fifty Six*
# White Knights

After a lifetime of thinking about this project and over fifteen years of active searching, I have learned a lot about Larry, airplanes and World War II. But, bottom line, did not find Larry or his airplane.

It's unfortunate that my mother knew his friends who were still alive during my adult lifetime, but shut them out just as she shut me out on the issue. Even if they didn't have any information about his disappearance, they could have given me more insights about him so I could get to know him as a person.

This was tragic.

Also, most of the other people who might have been in his life have passed on.

My mother could have introduced me, but she didn't.

At this stage, after hours of research and thousands of dollars in personal investment I came to realize that I am in over my head on this project. I need a partner with the financial resources and government connections to make this happen.

Several years ago I wrote to the top four billionaire executives of a major Internet search firm. After all, search is about connecting people with information and people with people. I sent four separate letters to four separate individuals with my press clippings and web information by DHL, but never got a reply.

Several months later, I saw that the firm ran a TV commercial about a child from India who had been adopted by a white Australian family but was driven to find his birth parents.

He used this particular Internet search firm to find them and the small village in India where they lived then surprised them with a visit. It was a joyous reunion.

Obviously, they stole my idea.

But there are other patrons who could make one person's dream come true. I need to find those patrons. According to what I've seen in the press over the last year or so, it seems that a lot of billionaires have made a hobby out of finding missing World War II wrecks. I was always trained to be independent against all odds, so was always embarrassed about asking people for help or money. Maybe it's time to change that strategy.

As Richard Hughs said, "You're only as good as your friends."

## *Epilogue*

For many years, a number of people pushed me to write this story, but I delayed and delayed, because I wanted a resolution, preferably with a happy ending. I had hoped that the significant amount of newspaper coverage in the U.S., Europe, French Guiana, Suriname, the Caribbean and even Hong Kong, would draw someone out of the woodwork with information or at least knowledge of Larry. However, the mystery remains unsolved and in the meantime Grammy, my Mom, Patricia's father, Ted Kaufman and Hugh van Es have all passed away. Meanwhile, my own health has taken a turn for the worse and had to have heart surgery. So maybe there are, in fact, powerful evil forces at work as the psychic said. While writing this book, I even accidentally stepped on my Timex Ironman watch and broke it beyond repair. Fortunately, I was able to buy another one, but obviously it was not the one that survived the jungle with me.

A friend suggested a heart attack could be the best thing that happened to me because I'd meet Larry in heaven and fulfill my lifetime search to find him.

An old girlfriend whose father flew P-40s with the "Flying Tigers" in China during World War II once said that her father claimed that "suicide is the coward's way out or the hero's way in." We broke up, so I don't know how it worked out for him, but he was very tormented and may have taken "the hero's way in."

Well, I'm not all that enthusiastic about any of those options and note from a logical standpoint, that if there is a heaven, then it's already probably filled with millions and millions of people, and I'd just have to start my search all over again there.

When I was in French Guiana and walking back from the village of Saül to the airfield for the return flight to Cayenne, I passed a small hut.

A woman had a cooler out front stocked with soft drinks buried in ice.

Cold drinks were a luxury in the rainforest, and I immediately grabbed a cold Coke.

"Please sign my guest book," she said as I was slowly savoring the soda.

"I heard about your story on the radio," she noted. "You need to sign my book."

She gave me a pen, and I prepared to sign my name. But before I put pen to paper she stopped me and said.

"You cannot just sign your name," she noted. "You must say something."

I didn't feel I had anything to say. Then out of nowhere, a short verse came to mind:

> *On and on we search,*
> *Sometimes, we find a little something,*
> *Most times we find nothing,*
> *But at least we find a little peace in searching.*
> *Peter Boczar*
> *French Guiana, July 1998*

## *Press Links*

My quest has received a fair amount of press coverage around the world. Below is a selection of links:

*CNN*
http://edition.cnn.com/2014/03/25/world/asia/malaysia-airlines-b24-mystery/

*The New York Times*
www.nytimes.com/2009/05/21/nyregion/21towns.html?_r=0

*The Trentonian, New Jersey*
www.trentonian.com/article/TT/20090524/NEWS/305249980

*The San Diego Union Tribune*
www.sandiegouniontribune.com/news/2009/aug/19/nephew-quest-pilot/

*NJ.com*
www.nj.com/news/index.ssf/2009/05/relatives_of_missing_world_war.html

*The South China Morning Post, Hong Kong*
www.scmp.com/article/475275/executive-deathbed-vow-and-warplane-downed-french-guiana

www.ingramcontent.com/pod-product-compliance
Lightning Source LLC
Chambersburg PA
CBHW060821050426
42453CB00008B/533